A Principle of
Recovery

A Principle of Recovery

An Unconventional Journey Through the Twelve Steps

Jack Grisham

Cover Design: Julia Kwong

Edited by Dyanne Gilliam / Katie MacKinnon

Proofreading: Elizabeth Lyle

Interior layout: Iris Berry

Copyright 2015 Jack Grisham

ISBN 978-0-692-52053-6

Acknowledgements

At some time in 1988 I was given this message, "You've got a problem." I didn't believe it at the time, but the carrier, Paul F., introduced me to a new way of life.

Other Works By Jack Grisham

An American Demon / 2011 ECW Press

Untamed / 2013 Punk Hostage Press

Code Blue / 2014 Punk Hostage Press

I Wish There Were Monsters / 2015

Contents

A Letter from Brother Paul

The Priest that Tastes the Word

"You never told me I was an alcoholic, or that I had a problem or that I needed help. You watched me drink and didn't drink and went to meetings and came back with a strange glow laughing about "the great meeting" you had just attended in Denver or Houston or Atlanta...while I stayed back at the club knocking back tequila shots congratulating myself that I had kicked my crystal meth habit—at least for a couple of weeks.

You showed me that "sober" could mean brazen, unapologetic, hilarious, kingly, free; psychedelic and manic and tragic and heroic. That there was nothing to miss from that benighted period I had left behind. That everything I had done or been drunk or loaded I could still do and be, that it had all been a lie, part of the gigantic tale we are told from birth, that we could party and buy our way to oblivion and not have been robbed of our one precious life.

You questioned the dogma in the rooms and it affirmed that there were no leaders, no rules, no authorities; that no one could kick us out. From you I learned to ask what I could bring to the meeting, not take away, and that meetings needed what we had, because institutions ossify and become rote and need a constant influx of visionaries and revolutionaries or they die, mindlessly uttering the same phrases and slogans over and over even after they had lost their power and even become offensive.

You walk through life with your anarchist eye, guided by love. You may have felt fearful and doubtful and sad and angry...but what you wore was fearlessness and freedom, irreverence and the deepest reverence imaginable. Yours is the ferocious certainty that YOU ARE HERE, tempered by the knowledge that even that isn't enough when we are only here for ourselves. That being so enormous as we are, for all intents infinite, with the capacity to create this universe we live in because IT IS OUR CHOICE...yet we shrink to a point of nothingness when we don't reach out to the other infinite souls and create this web of us.

Thanks Jack. You touched me a one eighty that spun another hundred out from me. You must have touched millions."

Paul R. Los Angeles 2015

A thank you to the one who may or may not be...

iv

Before We Go Further

I'm not claiming membership in any specific twelve-step program—that would be a violation of those programs' traditions, but most of my experience has come from the study of the Big Book—as it's been so lovingly called. I also acknowledge a very heavy debt to the word-of-mouth transmittance of personal experience.—and, you might read things here that have been inadvertently borrowed—stolen if you will. My apologies are offered in advance.

There are some that try to learn recovery from just reading pamphlet or page—and that can be a great place to start for raising awareness—but until you actually attempt to *practice* what you've read, you're traveling in fantasy land. You can't get wet from merely touching the word "water".

One day, just for the hell of it, I Googled, "How to have sexual intercourse." The result was interesting. I got a very clear and concise definition detailing the act of coitus. Here's an excerpt: "As humans become sexually excited, the sex organs prepare for coitus through changes in the circulatory and nervous systems. The brain receives signals from the genitals. The heart hastens flooding the arteries, the veins constrict. At the same time, blood engorges the erectile tissue of the penis and clitoris, as well as the testicles, ovaries, and labia minora."

Wow...I know I'm aroused.

The definition was clear, precise, and to the point, but it told me nothing of the taste of her lips, the feel of her hand in mine, the trouble I had in removing her bra, and the soft weight of her when she climbed onto my lap. It was textbook precision and basically worthless—especially, if I was looking for advice on my first trip to that wonderful world of carnal knowledge.

There are some that treat the Big Book only as a textbook. They can cite line and verse, memorize passages, and quote page numbers like a savant, but what of it? Yes, the Big Book is loaded with important information. Yes, if you attend twelve-step meetings, I'd suggest you study it. I've led a Monday night book study for the last eighteen years and we go through that book line by line. We start at the forwards, work through to pg. 164, and then we repeat; the last time it took us two and a half years to get through it, but that book is no holy relic. There's no pixie dust that will fly from those pages and twinkle you into sobriety, and there are many who are no longer with us that knew the ins and outs of those words better than I ever will. Sobriety is not a questionnaire, a line, or a lecture; it's an adventure, and the twelve-steps are a journey into the world of the spirit. You can't distill this voyage down to a single word; it's action, and each person's path is entirely their own.

Forward

Generally, people in recovery can't stand not knowing what's going on, and the majority of them think that there has to be a scam hidden somewhere within the program—somebody is profiting somehow, nobody offers anything worthwhile for free. Take our steps for example: I've always thought we should hide them. In most meetings they're displayed on large murals behind the podium. A new person walks in, sees free literature and our program shamelessly festooned upon the walls and they figure it can't be worth anything—the good shit is always hidden. I once suggested a new service commitment to the group: "the briefcase guy". We take the steps off the wall, remove the literature from the racks, and employ a man to stand in the back wearing dark glasses and holding a briefcase—inside are contained our pamphlets, our book, and our steps. The briefcase guy says nothing as the new people file in. They take their seats. The meeting starts. The topic is about, well…whatever, some negative aspect of life that a new person is wallowing in; let's say self-pity, that's a good one. We don't mention anything about the outstanding quality of our lives or how we got to this point.

One of the newcomers raises their hand, "Who's that guy?" they ask, referring to the man in back, "and what's in the case?"

"Don't you worry about the case," we say. "It's none of your business. As a matter of fact he's going to lock that case in the trunk of his car once we get going. Now, let's talk about depression."

The meeting continues, the mood spiraling downward…but the new person's attention is being drawn to what they can't have—the hidden goods.

"But what's he got?" they whisper. "What's in the case?"

"It's nothing," we reply, "it doesn't concern you."

As the meeting lumbers on—the briefcase guy having sequestered the goods—one newcomer after another sneaks away into the parking lot until a group of them are congregated around the car that conceals the mysterious item. A crowbar is found. The trunk is forced open. The briefcase is torn apart at the seams.

"It's the steps!" one yells, "and a book. I knew they were hiding something."

"They didn't want us to have good lives," another says. "They didn't want us to succeed. Screw them. Let's take these steps!"

Ah, if only I was in charge…

So, the questions you, as a reader, might ask me now are: "What are you doing? What's with this book? Are you trying to rewrite the program? Are you trying to profit off your sobriety? Who do you think you are?"

Well, I'll tell you. My name is Jack Grisham, recovered alcoholic, and I've been profiting off of my sobriety since I first became aware of the gravity of my situation and put a positive blueprint of living into action. I have a great relationship with those around me. I'm happily married. I enjoy life. I do the things I've always wanted to— the pleasures of a child enacted with the discipline of a grown-up— and I'm free. If that isn't profit, I don't know what is. As for this book, I'm not trying to rewrite anything. I have a few friends who are uncomfortable with the "God" issue, and some of the terminology in the Big Book—mainly, the sexist, antiquated slant—

and I'm hoping to be helpful, to loosen things up a touch so the door to the world of the spirit can remain wide open. I've been clean and sober a little over twenty-six years and this book highlights some of the perspectives that profoundly changed me—insights that have altered my perception of life and human connection. I've benefited from a drastic shift in philosophy and a new outlook on living and it pains me not to share these thoughts with you. I hope you enjoy this book and find in it some useful tools to rearrange any negative attitude on existence that you might be harboring; because after all, when it comes right down to it: your pleasure, your happiness, and your take on life, are all your choice.

x

A Room

We start with a room. For some of us it's a church basement, for others, an Alano Club or a well-appointed rehab, and for others still, the room is in a hospital or a prison. Wherever it is, this is where we make our introduction to the twelve-step program; but first, we meet the room.

The place where I began was filthy. The linoleum on the floor might have been light grey at one time but now it closely resembled asphalt, chipped and worn by the stumbling foot traffic of drying-out drunks and pacing-addict madness. There were couches, or at least that's what they used to be—dirty, cast-off, living-room lepers that were declined by the Salvation Army and ended up residing here. The first time I sat down, I worried about catching crabs. The walls were yellow—or at least the residue from a million smoked-to-the-filter cigarettes had made them so—and large roll-down vinyl murals of the twelve steps and the twelve traditions were hung with reverence at the front of the room, but these relics were also torn and well-used. This place was the poster child for seedy and I haven't even discussed its occupants. The heartbreaking crew that attended this gathering place were what looked to be passed-over extras from the film, One Flew Over The Cuckoo's Nest: crazies that were too unstable to live a so-called "normal" life. They were old and very young, in their late seventies to early teens, and there were boys and girls, men and women. They were a mix of inner-city black and white trash suburb. If there were those that came from well-to-do families, it wasn't mentioned here; some addicts and alkies want to live the life of the society victim, and a large trust fund takes something away from the tortured, young, street-punk vibe—the terminally cool we called them. There was also a cadre of Latinos and Longshoremen—all seemingly proud to be dying of alcoholism.

The bottom line is: this is what I saw, or, what I was capable of seeing at the time. I thought this room was my future, the destination of a journey unwittingly devoted to self-destruction. These people were the reflection of my life, and this is where my great dreams had led me. This was the end of my road...the realization made me want to kill myself.

The other day I was in a meeting, in a room quite a few degrees nicer than the one I just described. The space used to be an old beach bar a short walk from the sand. While it wasn't holiday chic, it wasn't bad either; it was a room with close to a hundred mismatched chairs and three or four rows of folding tables laid out in trying-to-be-straight lines. The walls were covered with knotty-wood paneling and there was a semi-clean carpet on the floor. In the back of this one-room hall was a small coffee bar and a set of his and hers restrooms—these were also fairly clean. I didn't worry about contracting a social disease or a parasite while I was there. It was a small, comfortable, beachside clubhouse—a one-room sobriety studio, if you will. Anyway, I was there to watch one of my mentors accept a forty-six-year medallion—recognition for almost a half-century of continuous sobriety. There were about thirty other alcoholics there, and one new man—a newcomer they're called—one of the thousands of beginners that walk through our doors seeking help. I didn't know whether this new man was there by choice or by decree—some of our beginners are pushed into our rooms by concerned family or friends, some by the threat of losing a job, some by the order of a judge, and some because they seek relief from themselves. Whatever his reason, he was new and I watched his eyes as he tried to accustom himself to the nature of his surroundings. When my mentor was introduced and claimed his forty-six years of sobriety, I watched the new man's facial expression drop to a visible level of defeat; his thoughts were as blatantly displayed as the slogans hanging on the walls of this club...but instead of "Easy Does It" and "One Day at a Time", his crushed countenance read: "Are you fucking kidding me? Forty-six years and this old dude is still sitting here? I'm fucked."

The new man's expression was created by the absence of hope. His plan of getting a "quick fix", and jumping back into the mainstream of life, was shattered. I read his mind,

"Look at this old man, sitting in that chair, forty-six years, grinning like a fucking idiot as these tired old lifers pay homage to him. Oh, my God, this room is a fly trap stuck to the bottom of a dead-end road."

I could only smile, for I saw my previous self in him.

Why belabor the point about the meeting room and how the newcomer might be reacting and absorbing it all? Did we really need every minute detail of the first shit-box I'd wandered into? Did I really have to describe the clientele and the condition of the toilets? I'm sure you quickly understood that the rooms were small and dirty and that the occupants were crazed and appeared to be going nowhere. Why put an almost negative connotation on what we might see? I do this because when we're new that's usually all we can see: the physical confines of a space and the temporal beings that occupy it. At this point we're incapable of realizing that the room has no walls and that the space not contained is the universe around. Some of these supposed "trapped" men and women—my mentor

3

included—have travelled distances that we'd only dreamed of; their life adventures, countless as the stars, have led them deeper into a range of emotional experiences than many of our greatest artists have ever touched...but when new, most of us are incapable of seeing that possibility. We can't see the great blessings that have materialized in these men and women, we can't see where this path of the spirit could take us; we can only see the room.

The Bear

He was the featured roadside attraction: a scarred old black bear that the gas station's owners had kept in a cage the last ten years. The cage measured six feet across and eight feet deep—rusty bars and straw on the floor. His owners fed him, and they housed him but he was never taken from the cage. He was an oddity and a prisoner.

Day after day, families, while on their journeys, would stop for gas and snacks and the children would crowd around the bear's cage. They yelled at him, poked at him with sticks when he wasn't looking, and at times, they threw things at him. When the bear was younger he'd growl and roar at his tormentors but these days, he accepted their taunts and their abusive behavior with depressed resignation. He would stand in his cage, ignore his onlookers, and walk in a tight regulated pattern—six feet up, turn, four feet to the right, turn, six feet to the back, turn, four feet to the right. Over and over he walked—a rectangle within the cage, taunted from outside, resigned to his fate. He would have died there had he not been released.

One day, an animal rights activist came by and witnessed the sorry state of that old bear. The activist was sickened by the lack of compassion shown, and led a successful campaign to free the animal. The bear was rescued and taken to a beautiful sanctuary in the mountains. There were streams and tall pines, fresh clean air, good food, and above all, a chance of peace.

When the bear arrived, his transportation cage was set down lightly in a clearing. The door was opened and he wandered from his confines. There were miles on either side that he could travel—a world to explore. The bear raised his head, took a deep breath of cool mountain air and then he walked six feet up, turned, walked four feet to the right, turned again, and walked six feet back—over and over, until he died.

The Bedevilments

Sometimes a true beginning doesn't originate in wanting something new; rather, it can come from being aware of the situations and the manifestations in our lives that we don't want. One of my favorite passages from the Big Book is affectionatly known as "the bedevilments."

"We were having trouble with personal relationships, we couldn't control our emotional natures, we were a prey to misery and depression, we couldn't make a living, we had a feeling of uselessness, we were full of fear, we were unhappy..." BB pg. 52

In the above passage, Bill W., the author, speaks solely of our emotional lives—he infers nothing of our drunkeness or our drug use. Bill dives directly into our relationships with the world around us, for after all, the drugs and the alcohol were but a symptom of the problem. They were our escape from a planet that had somehow turned against us. When we removed the symptom, the world remained hostile and unforgiving. So, let's break these "bedevilments" down.

"We were having trouble with personal relationships..."

Take a moment to reflect on the nature of your personal relationships. If you are married, how are things between you and your wife, or your husband—is it a loving bond? Is your relationship one of open communication, partnership, and trust? If you are dating or in a long-term situation, I ask you the same: do you have a shared vision or goal, or are you selfishly using others for quick comfort or pleasure? Also, don't forget your "exes"—how did those relationships terminate, and is there anyone whom you wouldn't want to run into at the market or when walking down the street? And these are just our romantic entanglements—how are your relationships with your friends, family, co-workers, bosses, employees, neighbors, teachers, and those various other people around you? Are you a giving, kind, open and honest person, willing to share and receive? Or, are you one who creates strife and mistrust, an architect of drama constructing great cathedrals of confusion and hurt? Perhaps you do "all that you can" (Saint You) generous to a fault, yet you still don't receive the desired result because of your selfish, controlling expectations of those around you...expectations that will likely never be met. Our "personal relationships" are characterized by our casual or intimate interactions with others. So, ask yourself: are these relationships supportive, respectful, and healthy...or not?

When I arrived at the door of twelve-step recovery I had warrants out for my arrest, I had people trying to kill me (both real and imagined), I got a girl pregnant and moved her into my mom's house and, at the same time, I fell in love with another woman (of questionable age) and I took her to Mexico and I married her. Was I having trouble with my personal relationships? Not at all, I was successfully pissing-off, terrorizing, frustrating, and angering practically anyone I came in contact with. No problem there. The interesting thing was this behavior was commonplace for me. I saw nothing wrong in the way I was living.

8

"We couldn't control our emotional natures…"

What are our emotional natures and why would we need to control them? The Merriam-Webster dictionary defines an emotion as, "A conscious and subjective mental reaction toward a particular event, usually accompanied by changes in the physiologic and behavioral aspects of a person." Additionally, when someone is characterized as "highly emotional" they are said to be, "Determined or actuated by emotion rather than reason".

In other words, thoughts lead to actions, or reactions in many of our cases, and not always in a positive way. Those of us who struggle with our emotional natures—for example, throw fits and have temper tantrums—take drastic action out of fear or anger, and basically run our lives by the often-unrealistic ideas stimulated by an "out-of-control" emotional system.

No one is expecting you not to feel sad or angry, not to feel trust or joy; these are normal human emotions that are crucial for adaptation and survival. If you didn't have these feelings you wouldn't be human. But what happens when these emotions are out of control, when anger becomes rage, when sadness becomes depression, when trust is misplaced or misgiven, and when joy becomes mania? How does it feel when you receive an unpleasant surprise, or when things don't work out your way? How do you react to the word "no", or when someone says, "You're going to have to wait"?

Emotions help us communicate our needs to each other, but in doing so, are our emotions a) screaming at the world around us, attempting desperately—even futilely—to express our wants? Or b) are we communicating these emotions in a rational, constructive

9

manner, and are we capable of entering a healthier world of reason, before we react?

After I'd been sober some time I realized how sad it was that people weren't always willing to tell me the truth. They were afraid. I reacted so violently when things didn't go my way that the bearer of unpleasant news thought himself or herself in danger for the delivery. In the Big Book, Bill writes that we'll learn to pause when agitated...funny, before I worked a program I was always a pause *after* agitated guy. "Sorry about your car man—don't call the police." My emotional nature was basically that of a savage.

"We couldn't make a living—"

Some of us have trouble getting, or maintaining a job, and others of us wish we could leave the job we're stuck in. But is "making a living" simply that, an ability to pay your bills and satisfy your material wants? One of the definitions of "alive" is: "to be active, alert, energetic, vigorous, vital and spirited." Do you exhibit those traits? Those of us who had trouble holding jobs often had problems with discipline or authority. If we were capable of cleaning ourselves up and presenting ourselves to a future employer, we could get the job, but could we hold it? Some of us would come into collision with our co-workers and, when we did, whom did we blame? Was it really the manager or the boss who was unreasonable or demanding, or was it our inability to work with a team, being one part of a collective whole? For those of us that could hold a position, did we feel "put upon, ill-used, and underappreciated"? Did we have dreams for something better, clinging to the thought that, "one day I'll be gone—retirement, its only another fifteen years..." And then there

10

are those who put all their energy into their work, leaving practically nothing of themselves for the people who care for them, or for whom they care for. Is this really a design for living the so-called "good life"?

In the movie *Runaway Train* there is a wonderful scene between two convicts that have recently escaped from prison. They're on a train speeding for what they think is freedom when the older convict (played by John Voight) asks the younger prisoner (Eric Roberts) what he plans to do when he escapes to freedom—I paraphrase here:

"I'll tell you what I'm gonna do, man," the younger convict says. "I'm gonna go to Vegas and party with the ladies."

"No you're not," the old veteran of crime replies, "you're going to get a job, a shit job, something a convict can get, maybe scrubbing floors and, one day your boss is going to come in and he's going to say 'you missed a spot' and you're gonna get down on your knees and you're not going to look him in the eyes and you're going to scrub that spot."

"Oh fuck that," the young one says. "I can't do that, man."

The old convict shakes his head and says, "That's your trouble, youngster. If you could do that, you could rule the world."

I was one of those that couldn't keep my mouth shut. I knew better than the boss. I thought I was better than you and I was doing you a favor by being your employee. But I lacked the discipline and the humility to succeed. If my job was to walk out to my parkway and pick-up a ten-thousand-dollar check once a day, I'd be fine for two weeks, and then I'd call the boss and say, "Why can't you just

11

put it in the mailbox—it gets wet out there." After two-weeks of a check in the mailbox I'd call with a new complaint, "Can't you just give me one check? It's a fucking hassle rolling up to the bank with a month worth of paper—seriously." And after two weeks of that, I'd indignantly call and demand, "Why don't you stick that fucking check up your ass. I quit."

No one could please me, and I couldn't please myself. I thought the world owed me a living, but when it tried to deliver, I was incapable of receiving.

"We had a feeling of uselessness—"

In the book *Man's Search for Meaning*, Viktor Frankl describes his experience as a prisoner in a World War II concentration camp. He witnessed men and women around him surrendering to their perceived hopelessness, and he watched them die. His fellow prisoners had lost family, possessions, and their dignity—and in their minds, there was no reason to continue living. Frankl knew that without something—some purpose beyond what he had known—that he, too, would soon lose hope and succumb to the inevitable. In his previous life, Frankl worked as a psychiatrist, and so he decided that it would be his job to counsel those who were interred. He would practice his healing craft within the camp and although he, too, had lost the things he had loved, he realized his reason for living was to be of service to others and it gave him the will to survive. This man's story is, of course, extreme; most of us will never know the horrors he faced. However, as we have learned repeatedly from history: in the most trying times, great ideas and shifts in consciousness can arise. What do you live for? Do you believe that we are nothing more than beasts waiting to die, and that in our existence there is no meaning, and thus, no purpose? Do you feel worn out, tired, and uninspired? Is your life a sentence of existence, doing the "day to day," just trying to get by? What motivates you... and, is it enough to give you the impetus to truly live?

I used to have a noose hanging over my bed. In the morning, after I said my ritual greeting to the day, "Fuck. I'm still alive," I would look up at the noose and I'd smile.

"Should I go one more day," I thought, "or should I hang myself now?"

I was twenty-six years old and I was tired of life. The days held no promise. The past held no pleasure. I was alive, but...I wasn't living.

"We were full of fear..."

How many of us have ever taken the time to look within and see what we're really afraid of? If someone asks, we could easily recite those surface fears that we know, e.g., "I'm afraid of flying." "I'm afraid of heights." "I'm afraid of speaking in public." But what of those that lie beneath, the fears that drive us, often without our knowing? For example, being afraid that something or someone we love will be taken from us, or that we won't receive something or someone we feel we deserve. How often have we been unwilling to take a risk, explore new territories, and step outside our perceived comfort zones? Are we afraid to be ourselves, to speak, or hold back; are we afraid to show weakness or vulnerability, are we afraid to be genuine? Are we afraid to really love—willing to give all without the fear of being hurt? Are we afraid to leave a relationship, for the daily pain and drama of being together seems less terrifying than the fear of being alone? The bottom line is, when we take an honest look at our lives, how much does fear really drive us?

Fear is a survival instinct instilled in our species, but are we just meant to survive, or are we meant to thrive?

I'm not sure I would've understood it when I was newly sober, but I wish someone had explained the depths of fear to me. I listed a fear of dogs and of being smothered as the only fears I had. The reality was, fear was my chief motivator and, sadly, when I reached my inventory, I was more upset by the things I hadn't done than the ones I had. I regretted deeply not exploring the chances, loves, and experiences that were offered me. I was ashamed that my fears—up until that point anyway—had cost me a wondrous life.

"We were unhappy—"

Where are you—is this what you wanted or expected from life? Where have all your accomplishments brought you? Where have all your plans led you? Are you light-hearted, cheerful, pleased and content? Are you satisfied, smiling, radiant and untroubled? To be happy, truly happy, is an emotional state that is almost impossible to hide from those around us. We beam when we are happy and our deeds, work, and relationships reflect that light. Happiness has little to do with our accomplishments, although we feel some satisfaction when we achieve what we strive for. Happiness, fundamentally, is an inner knowledge—sometimes beneath conscious thought—that we are loved, that we love, and that no matter the circumstances, we were, are, and will be okay. Are you happy?

14

Rarely has any newcomer to the program looked over these bedevilments and said, "No problem here baby, I'm good to go". You wouldn't be seeking help if these troubles didn't apply to you. Looking at our lives can be a sobering and, at times, very depressing task; but the awareness of a problem is the first step in arresting and moving beyond the issues we are struggling with. If we don't know, or are unaware of where we stand in this emotional landscape, then how can we ask for directions? How can we receive help? Thus, we must first determine our position in our relationship with the world around us, however uncomfortable that may be, and then hopefully we will have the desire and the will to move on.

If You Want What We Have

"If you have decided you want what we have and are willing to go to any length to get it—then you are ready to take certain steps." BB Pg. 58

Just what do we have that you might want, and how far do you have to go to get it? In the last section, you hopefully became aware of the things that you don't want, but what could we possibly have to offer you—and are you currently capable of seeing the manifestations of those offerings in our lives? A new person is usually only capable of seeing the material goods—because that's how most of us have been raised. For example,

"Check him out. He's got a great house and a flashy car. He's really got it going on."

But, by comparison, it's not as easy to see the goods that the spirit provides. And, although some of us do achieve great wealth, the gifts of the spirit aren't always measured in tangibles. The gifts of the spirit go beyond the material world.

Many times in meetings a newcomer will hear the promise; "You will have a life beyond your wildest dreams."

"I don't know," the newcomer might say, "my wildest dreams, huh? Well, I dream big!"

I'm sure you do, but if you take a moment to think of the things you dream of acquiring, how many of those dream items are of the material world: grand mansions, expensive toys—money to burn? But what if we went beyond your "wildest dreams", as that above promise mentioned, beyond the world of the material, and into the universe of the spirit—to the fourth dimension? What if your wishes were 'to know a new freedom and a new happiness, to not regret the past nor wish to shut the door on it, to comprehend the word serenity and to know peace, to realize that no matter how far down the scale you have gone, to see how your experience can benefit others? What if you could have those feelings of uselessness and self-pity disappear, lose interest in selfish things and gain interest in your fellows? What if your self-seeking slipped away and your whole attitude and outlook upon life changed? What if fear of people and of economic insecurity left you and you intuitively knew how to handle situations that used to baffle you?' What if these now became your wildest dreams and, if they were, how much would they be worth? When closely examined, such desires are so much more powerful than the desires of material wealth, because the dreams of the spirit encompass, yet also transcend, the worldly wants of man. Thus, these wildest dreams are unbreakable and no one can take them from you.

When I was new to the program and first attending meetings, there was a man who frequently sat across from me. He was older, he'd been sober some time, and had a look on his face that reminded me of someone who'd just eaten dinner. It was a slightly satisfied smirk that he wore—it was attractive, and he wore it more often than not, in times of good or bad. One day I commented on it.

"You always look so fucking satisfied," I said. "What's with it? Are you always happy? …Are you on something?"

He laughed. "Of course not," he said, "but I work a program and I trust in God. What is, is, and what will be, will be."

It was over my head at the time, but now that I often wear that same satisfied grin I realize what he meant. Those "wildest dreams" that we just spoke of, they can be found on pp. 83 and 84 in the Big Book, and they are promised to you—*if* you do the work. Anyone can be happy when they get what they want, but what if you could be happy regardless of whether things went your way or not? These promises are what we, those who have worked these certain steps, have experienced in our waking lives, and when you compare what we have to the life you probably identified with in the bedevilments, how far do you think you're willing to go to achieve it—how about, to any lengths?

To Concede and Admit

When starting this journey, many of us believe that the first step of recovery is admitting that one is an alcoholic however; there is much work that needs to be done *before* we can make that admission. There is a step before the steps, "Step Zero" it's been called, although it packs more weight than all of the other steps combined. This is the step of our awakening and, I believe, it's the most difficult, as well as the most painful to take. "Step Zero" is where we learn, mainly through our failures, that we are not connected to a power greater than ourselves, especially when it comes to our alcoholism.

"We learned that we had to fully concede to our innermost selves that we were alcoholics. This is the first step in recovery." BB pg. 30

How long, and what does it take to fully concede? For most of us, it takes years of painful existence before we can see the truth and, sadly, for some of us, we lose our lives before we awaken. This "Step Zero" is where we do the most damage to those around us; it's where our illness affects all who love or care for us; it's where we make decisions and take actions that will haunt us for years. It's where we lose loved ones, careers and relationships; it's where we destroy marriages and often take lives. And, as with most of the other steps, "Step Zero" is a process that no one can help us with—alcoholism is the only disease that has to be self-diagnosed, or fully conceded to, before you can begin to receive treatment. People might have told us, or suggested, that we're alcoholic; indeed, many of us have been talked down to, yelled at, punished, and discarded, because of our illness; but it's not until *we* look at our lives, sum up *our* actions, and diagnose *ourselves*, that we become willing to seek help, or even entertain thoughts of treatment. How many times do we have to screw up before we're able to see this crucial step of our journey? How many times do we have to fail? I wish I had an answer for you, but I don't, and no one else does either. There is no formula to awakening. One plus one does not equal two in the world of the alcoholic. You take one man, send him to jail, disrupt his life, and bring him pain, and in the morning he comes to, sees himself for what he has become, and moves forward with a willingness to change. You take another man, with the same exact circumstances, throw him in jail, disrupt his life, bring him pain, and in the morning he comes to and says, "Those cops are pricks and you've never understood me." There seems to be some sort of a psychic padlock guarding the mind of the alcoholic and the combination for awakening is different for each of us. Let's go back to the dictionary and take a look at one definition of alcoholism and what it is to be an alcoholic. Maybe it will help us gain some clarity. "Alcoholism is a chronic, progressive, potentially fatal psychological and nutritional disorder associated with excessive and usually compulsive drinking of ethanol and characterized by frequent intoxication leading to dependence on or addiction to the substance, impairment of the ability to work and socialize, destructive behaviors (such as drunk driving), tissue damage (such as cirrhosis of the liver), and severe withdrawal symptoms upon detoxification."

Jeez, and I thought I just drank too much. It's no wonder that some of us might read a definition like that and not identify with the message—especially those of us with a mind that struggles to see the

22

truth. And in the end, that's what we're dealing with: a mind that struggles to see the truth, a mental illness, or type of insanity, if you will. Now, you might think the jump between the concept of awakening and insanity is too great, but if we look at pg. 37 of the Big Book, insanity is defined as: "…a lack of proportion of the ability to think straight…" That's it. Bill isn't saying that we're dressing up in chicken suits, or that we think we're Napoleon or some other such nonsense. He's saying, that when the facts are laid before us regarding our alcoholism, we're unable to clearly see the problem. Moreover, the strange thing is, many of us are intelligent and aware, we're great problem solvers, but in this context—recognizing the severity of our illness—our intellect and ingenuity become practically non-existent. When I was beginning my journey into recovery, I read that dictionary definition of alcoholism and here's how I broke it down—keep in mind that at the time, I'd been jailed for drunkenness, couldn't hold a job, was beginning to have health problems, and was basically a mess:

"Potentially fatal; meaning, not always, and not me, it's the other guy who'll die from this—idiots, or the elderly, who can't handle their booze. Excessive and compulsive—really, I think you need to define excess, and as for compulsion, I only drink when I want to. Driving while intoxicated? I live in Southern California and the public transportation system is a joke. When I get liquored up, I have places to go, and how else am I going to get there? Besides, I'm a better driver when I have a buzz on—I pay more attention to the road. Work, well, we'll leave that out of this, but "to socialize"…who goes out and doesn't drink? It's rude to not have a cocktail at a party, or at a bar. Booze makes socializing easier—my ass gets tight without a few drinks to loosen me up.

23

When I get a couple in me, I'm invincible. Besides, alcoholics don't look like me. They live on the streets. They drink cheap wine—and not because they like the taste. They're dirty and they smell bad. I'm not that."

As an alcoholic who struggled to see the truth, I was able "in my own mind" to tear apart the clinical definition of alcoholism, and I also didn't fit society's generic definition of what movies, books, and television portrayed an alcoholic to be; but I was unable to see myself for what I truly was—a man with a drinking problem. In other words, I was insane. But one day I stumbled upon a definition that I couldn't tear apart—it gave me no room to wiggle—it pinned me to the wall, and it brought me the needed clarity. It was the definition of what it was to be an alcoholic found in the Big Book.

"If when you honestly want to, you find you cannot quit entirely, or if when drinking, you have little control over the amount you take, you are probably an alcoholic." BB pg. 44

This definition challenged the generic trench-coated-bum cruising-seedy-alley-ways and looking-for-that-last "spider in the bottle" picture of an alcoholic—although it certainly didn't exclude it. It went beyond the stereotypical convict, the continuous drunken driver, the broken homemaker, the lush, and the barfly definition—although, again, it didn't exclude them. For me, this passage removed every preconception of what I thought an alcoholic was and it challenged me to answer two important questions: a) when you're drinking, can you control it? And, b) when you want to quit, can you quit entirely? It was that simple. Hmmm, how many times, or in how many ways, have you quit only to start again? Have you

24

ever been so sick from your drinking that you swore off—"That was it, the last time." But then, maybe after a week or two, or possibly longer, you absolved alcohol as the guilty party and you blamed your illness on the mixer, the color of the liquid, the brand name, or not properly fortifying your stomach before you got down, and so you drank again? Or maybe, the last time you quit had nothing to do with being sick at all, maybe you acted in a way that crossed your line of bad taste or morality—you embarrassed yourself. Maybe you woke up with someone you weren't too familiar with—someone you probably wouldn't have slept with if you hadn't been hammered. The regret lasted for a bit, but then the sting and discomfort shifted to the back of your mind...and with time, you poured yourself a little "nerve relaxer" or a "cold beer on a hot day". Have you ever put a few in you and then lost that wonderful inner-monologue that we all adore, and you end up putting words on the table that probably should have remained in your head?

"You know what, sweetheart? You're a real bitch and your chicken tastes like parrot."

A move like that could possibly tank your relationship—if she or he was healthy enough to leave, or it could just push your tail between your legs and have you cowering until you get some distance between you and your loose mouth...and then, you forget why you quit, or you excuse your lapse in manners, and you drink again. Whatever the reason (and I'm sure I could give you hundreds), at some point in our drinking and using careers we have probably quit before, for one reason or another, and yet we started again—we couldn't stay stopped—and as you might have experienced, such periods of abstinence don't have to be brought about by some great catastrophic failure like jail, homelessness, or

25

death. Indeed, these periods of abstinence can be the result of minor inconveniences; but whatever our reason for quitting, it was soon displaced by the powerful idea of taking a drink, because, as alcoholics, we can't seem to summon up the pain or the fear of the day before. Our embarrassment and hurt becomes nonexistent, and then we forget, and we do it again. So alcoholism, according to this definition, has little to do with, "why we quit" or "how much we drank", or "our social status", or "what was transpiring in our lives at the time", as much as it has to do with, "why couldn't we stay quit?" And then there's the second part of that Big Book definition, the control thing. I don't know about you, but when I was drinking I wasn't usually capable of just having one, a little nip before bed, or an aperitif before dinner. Sure, on the rare occasion I might have pulled off a one-drink night, but if so, it didn't last…my limited success in controlling my consumption soon turned into greater failures when I found myself doubling, tripling, or quadrupling that 'little taste'. When I got rolling, I usually didn't stop until the wheels came off.

Okay, so hopefully by now we're getting a touch of clarity, we're beginning to see where we have been insane—or lacked the ability to see the truth. We have learned a bit about our illness and the way it affects us, and those around us. We've gained knowledge of ourselves and our condition, and we should feel pretty good about that; now we're ready to pull ourselves up by our bootstraps and "get down to recovery"…but wait a minute, it's not that easy. We're about to touch on the most frightening aspect of this illness, encapsulated in the past-tense wording of the first step: that we were

26

powerless over our alcoholism. That presently, we are without power.

How badly do you want to live? How much do you care about the people around you? Do you want to have a good life, be successful in business, love, and family? Do you want to live without the pain and the heartache associated with your illness? Do you want to stay out of jail? Do you want to live free, not under the lash of alcoholism—with all your heart? Wonderful. Now, think of all you love, and all you want to achieve, and how much you want to have the best of all things and then...know this: it doesn't fucking matter what you want, and what you're going to lose if you get loaded again, or how hard you're willing to work, because if you have our illness— the disease of alcoholism—you're going out anyway, and there's nothing you can do about it. THIS is being without power. This is having an illness that tells you 'you're okay', that lies to you. This is the insanity. And beyond this, beyond your conscious reasoning of why "one more drink" *this time* will be different, is something else...it's called a "sober black-out" or a lapse in consciousness, and we find ourselves once more with a drink in our hands and no idea of how it got there.

"I saw that willpower and self-knowledge would not help in those strange mental blank spots. I had never been able to understand people who said that a problem had them hopelessly defeated. I knew then. It was a crushing blow." BB Pg. 42

The acknowledgment that no human power can help you is a realization of hopelessness. Knowing that even though we might

27

have just stepped away from a painful situation, or that we're still reeling from the heavy sting of the ruin that we've created, we're going to do this again, and again, and again, until we are left with no one, and nothing—and we have pulled down everything and everyone around us—we have succumbed to the illness with our lives. The disease of alcoholism is cunning, it is baffling, powerful, patient, and it is deadly—a fatal illness, which you cannot, by your own power, arrest...too bad for you.

If there weren't a way out, the Big Book would stop after Bill convinced us we were hopeless, or maybe continue on with a few blank pages before an "end date" is printed on the back cover, and hence that would be it—the end of our lives. But thankfully, there *is* a way out—although it's a desperate one. You must seek this path with the fervor of a drowning man seeking air: that is, with all your heart and desperation, because your very existence depends upon finding a power by which you can live.

A man in recovery once told me that each step inadvertently poses a question that is answered by the following step. When I am buried in my illness—oblivious to my disease, the answer is conceding to my innermost self that I am ill, that I'm suffering from alcoholism and that I need help. When I have conceded, or accepted that reality, the next step is to admit my illness, my powerlessness, and my inability to lead a manageable life. When I have conceded and admitted to that and I'm residing in utter hopelessness, the answer, according to the twelve-steps, is that I must come to believe in a power greater than myself...a power that can restore me to sanity, relieve my alcoholism, and give me a means and a purpose to live.

Looking back, it took me a year and a half of sobriety before I fully conceded. I remember the day. I was at a noon meeting. I had just gone surfing. I had a few dollars from my mother tucked into my pocket. I didn't have a job. I was living the life of the idle rich, although I was far from it. It was a beautiful afternoon, a light ocean breeze twisted through the trees. I grabbed a cup of coffee, two cookies (both a touch stale), I sat back in my metal folding chair, and I lit a Marlboro red. I was sober, but I was as clueless as the day I walked in. The meeting began. I don't remember what they discussed—at the time I thought more about what I had to say than what I could learn, and then the universe, or God if you will, sent me a message. It came in the form of clarity of thought. I stepped outside myself (figuratively, not literally) and looked back at what I was. I saw my past and became aware of how many times I had "gone straight" and then fucked it up again. I was the Pinocchio of alcoholism—I meant well, wanted to be a real boy, but I always ended up sucked into trouble, braying like a jackass on Pleasure Island. I saw the times that I'd quit drinking and then watched as I shook it off and poured myself another vodka with a Valium chaser. I saw the lying, cheating, and getting arrested again—after I'd told myself that the time before would be my last. It was then I realized that even though I was sober, and that my life was slowly improving, I was going to pull it down around me as I did countless times before…I was going to destroy myself. The realization was horrifying. I was rocketed into reality and it hurt. I wanted to scream. I sat up in my chair and I looked for someone to help me, but there was no one. The room was full with those in recovery but I knew that they weren't strong enough to stop my descension into the void. I realized that a "hero" sponsor couldn't help me, that

29

memorizing the Big Book would be futile, that ninety meetings in ninety days weren't enough, and I had no connection with the power needed to avert this human catastrophe. I knew one day I'd tell myself, "You've got this." "You don't need these people anymore." "You're fine. You can move on." Then, after a few weeks or months on my own, I'd say, "one drink won't hurt." I was crushed...my ego and thoughts of self-sufficiency were smashed.

I don't know if you've ever seen one of those extreme slow motion films of a ball being bounced on the ground—the ball falls to earth and it flattens as it hits, completely deflated...that's what I was. I fell and was crushed, flattened against the world, and for a moment I was as hopeless as a man could be...but only for a moment.

As If You Could Wake Them

When dealing with the world of recovery you will often come into contact with those who practice pride as if it were an asset. They collect "sponsees" as if they were dolls or plastic army men. They won't admit it, but they supplant a Higher Power by setting themselves up as God. They teach the newcomer to put their dependence on them, giving direction based on what *they think* that new person should be doing...instead of sharing their experience and then helping the newcomer find their own way. These older members say they "trust God", but they don't trust God enough to get out of the way and let God work. At times I hear these self-appointed demi-Gods say, "I make my men do a first step."

"Really? You make your man concede to his innermost self that he's an alcoholic? How the fuck do you do that?"

We can't make someone wake-up. We can't make them concede. If we could, you'd see me on T.V., wearing a sharkskin suit, flashing a million dollar grin, standing before a mansion with a stack of cold hard cash in my hand and telling the desperate public where they should go.

"Trouble with alcoholism? Not any more. For twenty-nine ninety-five I'll get your loved one to concede to their innermost self that they have a problem and they will seek help. Shit, just for today, I'm running a two-for-one recovery special. That's right, "Easy Does It" I'll get two of your most hopeless cases to wake up, seek help, and turn themselves around. Act now, a human is a terrible thing to waste..."

Sometimes I wish I had that power, and then maybe, my first wife, my nephew, my father, and a host of my closest friends, would still be alive.

Coming To Believe

That first step hit us pretty hard with the frightening, and hopefully sobering, reality that we have a fatal condition, and without some sort of spiritual, "Greater Power", or "God" connection, we're destined to drink or use again—regardless of what we try to do to arrest our urges—and I've found that to be true. However, what if, at this present time, you still don't believe in the "powerless" concept, or you can't as yet accept the depth and weight of your malady? Yes, you can still feel and see the repercussions of your latest debauch, and you're basically aware of your present location and what your drinking and using has cost you, but really…fatal, powerless, and insane? Those are harsh words. What if you're willing to give the twelve steps a shot, but you're not yet totally convinced that you're an alcoholic of "our type"? On pg. 31 of the Big Book, Bill suggests that if you're not sure you're one of us, go at it again—try some controlled drinking, and see how that works out for you.

"Well, screw that," you might reply. "I may not fully believe in the depth of my problem, but I'm not an idiot, and I'm definitely not willing, at this time, to go another round with what just thoroughly kicked my ass."

Many of us thought the same, myself included. I might not have been completely clear on what was going down—the gravity of my illness, but I wasn't about to step in the ring and take another beating.

"Powerless? …Maybe. Fatal? …Who knows? But my life is a mess, so yeah; I'm going to give this program a shot."

The good news is Step Two allows people like us to find our way into recovery and it gives us time to accept our condition.

"Came to believe that a Power greater than ourselves could restore us to sanity." BB pg. 59

The beauty of this step is that it operates in two directions simultaneously. It gives us an opportunity to come to believe in a healing power, and, it gives us a chance to disbelieve that which we thought would work for us—our "old ideas." In other words, as we take this journey of recovery, we gradually develop a greater understanding of our illness and, we also begin to see the Greater Power working within—and through, those around us.

One of the tenets of a twelve step program is that we must be helpful to others—a "servant leadership-based philosophy", and when we are beginning our recovery, and learning to be useful, we get the opportunity to stick a hand out to those newer than ourselves. It's in this process where the mirror—the reflection of our old behavior—is shown to us in the words and the actions of the new person; it is in this series of moments that we begin to recognize our illness in others.

When I was still fairly new, an attendee of the meetings called my home. I was upset at first. I didn't like him invading my personal space—*keep it in the rooms,* I thought, but I let him talk for a minute or two, I had nowhere to go. He told me that he thought his girlfriend was cheating on him. I asked him why.

"Because, I called her house and it was busy," he said, "and then I called this guy's house, the one I think she's digging on, and his phone was busy too."

"Did you try an emergency breakthrough?" I asked.

"Yeah," he replied, "it was declined."

I'm sorry for the archaic phone references, but this was in the 1980s and we didn't have cell phones. We had big plastic devices that weren't mobile. A busy signal was what you received when someone you were trying to call was using their phone—a nasty, squawk, squawk, squawk—and it was enough to make you blow your brains out; so an emergency breakthrough was when you asked the operator to call the busy party and clear the line so you could get through. When your "break-through" was declined, it meant the other party knew it was you, and they didn't care, they refused to hang up.

Anyway…I was listening to his paranoia and then, unwittingly, I was sucked in, "Yeah," I said. "I bet she is cheating on you. We should get a couple of cars and catch them in the act."

I paused in thought…and, as he was celebrating his newfound co-conspirator, I was taking a quick inventory of the situation.

"This dude is an addict," I thought, *"and an alcoholic of the worst type. I've heard him share in the group. I know him, and I know his illness, and I think just like him. I'm screwed."*

Now, as you can see, our conversation had nothing to do with drugs or alcohol, it was a conversation of paranoia, bad ideas, and fear. It was a conversation between two sick men who thought alike and shared this common thread of insanity and I recognized myself in him. I've done what he's doing. Through that conversation I caught a frightening glimpse of the alcoholic illness that centered in

35

my mind—I identified with his thinking, and I believed I was in trouble.

The longer I stayed sober, and spoke with others of my type; I heard more of myself in their words. At times, I heard stories of drinking and using that specifically paralleled my own, and at other times I heard tales of family troubles, of relationships in jeopardy. Sometimes the speaker would be aware that they were the true cause of the problem, and at other times the speaker played the role of a "victim" and the world was "doing it to them"—this innocent victim role was the one I most identified with, because at the time I was still learning that it was *I* who needed to change, not the world around me.

And then there were those who spoke to me with their deaths. I was surrounded with others who had this fatal illness and I watched many fail to recover. I saw them remain unaware—unwilling to participate. I watched them hang on to their ego with the desperation of those who would try to prove themselves non-alcoholic, even if it killed them in doing so—and it frequently did. The longer I stayed sober, the more they died. After several years of losing many friends and family members to this illness, I finally came to believe in the concept of powerlessness, and the ultimately fatal progression of my condition.

But, as I was learning death and insanity, I was also learning power and love. There was a young man who came into our group, he was haggard, fresh off the streets, and he fit the bill of a homeless junky wino: dirty, couldn't hold a job, and was as undesirable as a man could be. He was a cast-off from society, a pariah, and on his last days. He was hopeless. But miraculously, I saw him get a few days sober—shaky as hell, but hanging in. I watched people on the program help him find a place to stay, they got him fresh clothes, and they cleaned him up. He took a service commitment making coffee for the group and after meetings I saw him sweeping floors and straightening chairs. He got thirty days, and then sixty, and then ninety. He went back to school and reunited with a son that he'd walked out on years ago. I rarely spoke with him but I watched him change. One day he came to the meeting on his lunch break. He was wearing a nice suit. He was full of life and purpose. His destiny had somehow been changed. He had recovered.

I saw a power work through, in, and around this man—God, if you will—and by way of his transformation, and many like his, I came to believe.

You can tell me that there's a great power for good, and you can tell me that there's a fatal flaw in my make-up, but I won't really believe it until I see it, until I experience the situation first-hand. In my own journey of recovery I came to believe that I was fatally ill, that I was destined—without connection or awakening—to drink again; but I also came to believe that there was a power that I could connect to, one that would heal me and the world around me. It was to this power that I decided to turn my will and life towards.

For a moment, let's go back to that flattened ball—that crushed ego, that state of hopelessness. That feeling of utter defeat doesn't have to last long, but I believe you have to experience it, even if it's just for a moment. I was crushed that day, down for the count, done-for, and then I thought, "…*but they're doing it.*" These people are staying sober and, if I do what they do, follow those steps, then I too can recover." I believed in what I saw and I believed it would work for me.

37

There's an interesting bible passage—now, don't get alarmed, I'm not about to start rolling holy over your asses, but it applies here whether you believe in Christ or not. The story goes something like this.

A centurion had a servant who was sick. The man was dying. Christ was out teaching and performing miracles and the centurion went to him.

"Rabbi," he said, "my man is paralyzed and needs your help."

"Should I come to him?" Christ asked.

"No," the centurion replied, "I'm not worthy of that, but if you just say the word it will be done."

And then Christ said, "Go! Let it be done just as you believed it would." And his servant was healed at that moment.

Now, what I find interesting in this passage is the line: "let it be done as you believed it would."

It was the man's belief that healed the servant, not the power of Christ. Yes, I know this may sound like blasphemy and I'm sure my soul has just been hung over Hell on a S'more stick, but am I wrong? I believed that the people in the meetings were sober. I believed that if I did what they did that I would also recover—I didn't ask them to heal me or give me something I hadn't worked for. I was willing to put in the time, and I did it. As we'll soon see I had no usable understanding or knowledge of a God…and yet, it worked.

A quick moment of explanation, lest you be offended:

"Jack?"

"Yes?"

38

"You sure refer to the Christ a lot. Are you trying to push religion down our throats?"

"Of course not. I'm not a fan of organized religion, although I do like the incense and the robes. I am, however, a big fan of the teachings attributed to Christ and I refer to them quite frequently. At times it puts me in an awkward place: I'm basically a Christian-based agnostic who doesn't believe in "buckets-of-fish" miracles, or a heavenly afterlife. In being such, I upset some Christians by using what they consider blasphemous language and disregarding a majority of the Bible, while I often anger the secularists by mentioning a God they don't believe in. As Abraham Lincoln said, "you *can* piss off most of the people most of the time," or something like that. Thomas Jefferson was also a believer of my type—or me of his—so I put myself in fair company. Jefferson compiled a book titled, *The Life and Morals of Jesus of Nazareth*, which basically separated the teachings of Christ from the supernatural and the dogmatic trappings of the church. For example, in a 1813 letter to John Adams, Jefferson wrote: "In extracting the pure principles which he taught, we should have to strip off the artificial vestments in which they have been muffled by priests, who have travestied them into various forms, as instruments of riches and power to themselves...There will be found remaining the most sublime and benevolent code of morals which has ever been offered to man."

So, when I mention Christ, as I will do, please understand that I'm not trying to convert you, I'm simply sharing some basic principles that have helped me better understand the journey.

Feel Like Drinking?

I couldn't go through a day without thinking about it. When I felt sad, lonely, angry, frustrated, or sorry for myself, I'd think about getting high—taking a little something to ease my pain—a few Valium or an Ativan, a couple of cocktails, maybe some mushrooms, or a few pulls off the bong. I wanted relief. I used to tell people that I felt like getting loaded—constantly. I'd share it in meetings.

"I can't fucking take it anymore," I'd say. "I hate what sober feels like. I can't stand being here."

Waking up is hard. It hurts. Being rocketed into a reality that's an emotional wasteland is never pleasant—and I don't care how long you drank or used—because chances are you've made decisions and taken actions that you now regret. There's a funny story in the Big Book on pg. 82, it's about a man who comes out of the cellar after a tornado has destroyed his home—he's happy the wind has stopped blowing, but in reality, he's asleep. He's clueless to the damage. If I were to compare my life to a natural disaster it would be a tsunami—a tidal wave of craziness and destruction that engulfed all around me with its self-centered swirl. When I washed into the program it was atop a sea of lies, hurt, and pain, but I was oblivious to what lay beneath—the waters of insanity were covering the truth. At the peak of the destruction, I landed here, this mountaintop of recovery, and the wave began to recede—and, as it did so, it popped the bottle from my mouth, the pills from my hand, and pulled away the debris from my eyes. I was awake, and I wasn't happy. I was twenty-six years old. I lived at my mother's—couldn't take care of myself. I owed thousands of dollars in back child support. There were warrants out for my arrest. My father was dead. I had no plan, no scam, and no foreseeable way out. I was scared. The wreckage of the wave was vast. It hurt. I wanted relief. I wanted to get loaded...

I was listening to a young woman's story; she was shaking, softly sobbing as she related a tale of relapse, rape, incarceration and the death of her lover. It was heartbreaking. After she finished—a five-minute horror oration of degradation and destruction, she closed with, "I hurt. I don't know what I'm going to do. I feel like getting loaded."

Feeling like you want to get high is normal and expected. Alcoholics are notorious for wanting to wander into dreamland, "full-flight from reality" Bill called it, but wait...do you really *"feel"* like getting loaded?

"For most normal folks, drinking means conviviality, companionship and colorful imagination. It means release from care, boredom and worry. It is joyous intimacy with friends and a feeling that life is good." BB pg. 151

For most "normal folks"...like us? I've found that there are at least two definitions, or meanings, to every word or phrase. There is the literal definition, and then, there is the emotional one. If I asked a man to tell me what "father" meant, he could recite this: "A father is the male parent of a child," which is correct, but if I asked him to define what "father" meant to him, it would be quite different. If he had grown up with a father who was kind, loving, supportive and a strong leader, his definition would reflect those traits, but if he'd grown up with a father who was abusive, distant, drunken and unkind, his definition would be thusly colored. Now, if we look at "drinking", or what it is "to drink", the normal or, non-alcoholic man could give us the textbook definition: "drinking is the act of ingesting alcohol into the body through the mouth" and then, he could give us the other, the definition Bill gave, the one of conviviality, companionship and colorful imagination; the release from care, boredom and worry; the joyous intimacy with friends and that feeling that life is good. Yes, the "normal" man could recite those, but, as we hopefully have accepted, drinking *to us* doesn't mean that at all—we aren't normal in regards to our illness. Sure our technical definitions are the same, but our emotional definition is much different. To most alcoholics, drinking means being unhappy, separation, and bewilderment. It means obsession, chaos, and worry; loss of intimacy and suffering from a feeling that life is a punishment meant to be endured.

So now, when I look back at that young woman's story—and my own experience with "feeling like drinking"—I realize, that her emotional definitions of what it was to 'drink' or 'get loaded' hadn't changed. She was still thinking that drinking meant relief and freedom, when in reality—for her—it meant just the opposite.

When I said I felt like drinking, what I really meant was: I want to feel loved, companionship, relief, and comfort. I want to feel connected, confident, and secure. These were things that I'd never get from drinking or getting loaded. From those two agents I got slit wrists, fouled pants, and a trip to jail—three things that I definitely didn't want.

There used to be a sign hung from the walls at select clubhouses and it read, *"THINK, THINK, THINK."* Sadly, that placard is usually removed by those who don't understand; some confused "longtimers" who think it's cute and witty to tell you not to use your brain—not to think, as if they could save you by their "infinite wisdom". The actual founders of the twelve-step program wanted you to think—as we'll see later. That sign represents the concept of "thinking the drink through"—where would it take you if you did get it on? Next time you "feel like drinking", I'd suggest reframing your definition of what getting loaded means. It might avert a beating.

As We Understand It

How crushed are you? In a perfect world—or rather, in the pursuit of an elusive perfect program—it would be at this point in our journey that we find ourselves hopelessly defeated, that we've realized that no human power, no earthly connection, no scam, no plan, no foreseeable way out could possibly help us; more simply put, this is when our map of a world run on self-will becomes a dead-end. We would be at the point of giving up—a microsecond away from letting go of our lives, and it would be in this moment of total desperation that we'd drop to our knees and reach out to whatever God might be there—we'd cry for help. Yes, if we believed in God and, had full knowledge of our condition—of the fatalness, the hopelessness, and yet, still with a desire to live—this *is* when we would fully surrender and turn our lives over to the care of that Supreme Being, no matter what He, She, or It was, or stood for…at this point in our existence we would be convinced that a life based on selfish-will was futile, and that there was no other way out. Yes, in a perfect world, this is where we would be, and there has been many an alcoholic that has stood on the edge of that abyss—many times. I've heard it said in meetings that you can't scare an alcoholic, but that's a lie. Alcoholics are fear-based people, always thinking that we're not going to get what we want or that what we have will be taken from us, and we take actions based on those fears—they drive us. Alcoholics scare easily, but we forget just as quick. I've made quite a few fear-based decisions to go straight, to change my life, and to follow a spiritual path. At two or three a.m., when the blow is gone and the booze has run dry, when my girlfriend has left me,

45

when I've lost another job…sure, out of frustration and hurt, I'd give up. At times, crying in my room, I'd swear that this was my last dance, and that I was going to walk the straight and narrow from now on. But when the light of day hit my eyes, and the thought of a new plan to succeed came upon me, I'd forget all about that pledge; I'd shake off the demons of defeat and I'd put on my boogie shoes—I think the first time I went straight, I was in the third grade. There seems to be a period of surrender—a window opened by fear and pain in an alcoholic's life where we're willing to do anything to recover…but it's a very small window, and I've watched many beaten-down drunks offer up a desperate pledge to change and then, after no further action was taken on their part, that window of opportunity closes and they drift off to drink and use again.

If we look back over our lives, there might've been times that we vowed to stop getting loaded and change our ways, "temperance pledges" they used to call them, a promise made in a moment of defeat or concern: "I'll workout more; I'll stop eating shitty food; I'll quit sleeping with her, or him; I'll do better at work—really step up production; I'll quit drinking or using; I'll quit lying and cheating, I promise." These are all well-intentioned pledges, but most of them are motivated by fear, and how many of these plans are followed up with the action it takes to make them a reality…and if they were followed up, how long did the changes last? If your window is open, I suggest you jump through. Sometimes establishing a discipline when we're willing can carry us through the times when we're not.

There are two kinds of motivation: "away" and "toward". "Away" motivation is when we back away from trouble. You've heard the expression "the heat's on", and like holding a hand over a hot stove we recoil from the adversity. This "heat" is usually fueled by fear: of death or a health issue, divorce, jail, a loved one threatening to leave, or the imminent loss of a job. Heat fueled by fear is a wonderful motivator...but it doesn't last. When we're motivated by such heat, the impetus to succeed only lasts as long as the heat is on. When we're behaving in a positive manner, it's usually not long before we're once again trusted, not drug-tested or in jeopardy of losing our jobs, off probation, living the good life, and back in the big bed...when the heat fades, and we think the troubles are over, that the bogeyman of alcoholism and drug addiction has moved on to other victims. Now, if the heat was what propelled us, and it's no longer there, naturally we're no longer motivated to succeed; we end up settling down, forgetting about the hurt and the suffering of yesterday, and we begin to reengage in the behaviors that harmed us in the first place. This can lead to a terrifying cycle of burned, retreat, burned, retreat, and burned again—also known as a consistent string of relapses. I've seen some of us suffer through this process for years. It's heartbreaking. Recovering alcoholics who seem to be on the road to freedom stop doing the work, because to them their goals of being off probation, reunited with the ex, having a secure job once again, and so on, have been achieved, and there's seemingly no reason to continue with a program—they've got what they wanted.

The other motivation is called "toward" motivation, and this behavioral response is more in line with a twelve-step program. This type of motivation may start as "away", but at some point in our journey we stop backing away from the heat and we turn and walk toward the light—or an enlightened self-interest, if you will. This is by far the more successful of the two because "toward" motivation is beyond goal-based...that is, our end result is not a specific "thing"

47

or "outcome", rather it's an ideal—keeping in mind we never achieve perfection. In regards to recovery, we do our best to be useful loving servants of those around us, and in doing so, we benefit by the world's response to our good, or unselfish, will. We stop fighting to stay out of jail, and we practice actions that give us a life beyond reproach. We stop worrying about how to save our relationships, and we practice behavior that makes us a more attractive friend, partner, or lover. We stop fighting to save our jobs and we practice being cherished assets to our employers and companies. We stop patching holes in our relationships with our children, and we practice being parents who are admired, trusted, and loved. We work through and beyond the problems of the day, and yet we still recognize that there is always room for continuing improvement. With this route taken we are now moving in a direction of long-term, contented, useful sobriety, and our relationship with a power greater than ourselves is the key to that new life.

"Made a decision to turn our will and our lives over to the care of God *as we understood him.*" BB pg. 59

When I came to this point in the steps, I was mildly frightened and highly confused. I was being asked to turn toward something I didn't understand—and wasn't sure I believed in—and, when I did think of a Higher Power, it was a conception that was built on guilt and shame. I'd done some things that not too many people would be proud of. I had a picture in my mind of this ultra-conservative punishing sky-king who was itching to send me to Hell—he just hadn't gotten around to it yet. In my mind, turning my will and life over to the care of God meant I had to stop cussing, get a sales job at Sears, and not touch myself below the waist without a wash cloth. Thankfully, I wasn't afraid to share these thoughts in an open twelve-step meeting and I voiced my fears to a room full of laughter. I wasn't the only one who had harbored such nonsensical beliefs. A man approached me after the meeting. He asked me if I knew what "my will" was and if I had a handle on the definition of "my life." I didn't. He explained that my will was my thoughts, and my life was my actions—as if that did me any good.

"Learn to think like us," he said. "Follow our actions. Work your steps. Stay clean and be of service—your understanding will come." It was a touch cult-like and I had no intention of handing out pamphlets at the airport.

"What about 'self-will' versus 'God's-will,' and all that other crap?" I said. "There's no denying it. The word 'God' is written all over those steps."

"Yes, you're right," he said. "But it's *your* understanding of God; we don't make you believe anything. You choose your own conception."

"Well, what if I choose to believe that God is a joke?"

"Believe what you want, kid. But are you comfortable with that? Is that a concept you can use?"

"What do you mean 'use'?"

"I mean can you turn to it, count on it, and grow from it? Is that a loving conception? Is there power in that?"

"No, not really, but it's…uh…"

"What do you think of when you think of 'Him'?" he asked. "What's your understanding of God and 'His' acts?" I described the God I'd envisioned and I told him of the torture in which I was existing—my world was basically crumbling at the edges—living at my mother's, no car, no prospects, couldn't hold a job, broke, owed back child support...and was basically a mess.

"God has done a number on me," I said, and then I smiled. "I'm suffering the tortures of the damned—the tortures of the damned."

"God did that to you, huh?" he replied. "Son, I'm going to make a guess that you never made a decision that wasn't going to benefit you. I'll go as far as to say that you probably thought of no one but yourself in the majority of your actions. You probably went for comfort every time—a quick fix or relief. Think about it. Did you ever sit quietly before acting...and really think about how your moves would affect those around you? Were you ever willing to be uncomfortable in the moment in order to gain long-term comfort?"

"Huh?"

"That's what I thought. Let's look back at your conception of God and, just for a moment, let's think of God differently, like a loving Father, or Mother—a parent who is concerned for all their children, including you. This would be a definition of God's will, or God's thoughts—from an all-inclusive, kind, loving protector who took the whole human family into consideration when they acted; also, this parent lets you act as you wish regardless of how your actions could harm you...they don't punish you, you punish yourself by the world's reprisals to your selfish or unthinking behavior."

"Are you saying that I did this? I created this mess?"

"Yes, I bet if we looked back over your life we could trace every problem back to an action you had taken that was based on selfish thought or self-will, and yet, I've heard you share, you're quite the victim."

50

"I was abused," I told him. This was a defense I often went to. "Are you saying that was my fault? I created that?"

"No—you didn't create the abuse, but you sure as hell have played that victim role down to the last card. You allowed what they did to rule your life."

He was right. Every problem in my life could be traced to a self-seeking action that I had taken, and when possible, I played the victim—"It was them, they're doing it, not me."

"If you remain the victim," he said, "things are never going to get better until they—the ones offending you—stop, or come clean and apologize for their past behavior. If you're willing to recognize and accept that you've been the problem, you now have a way out."

"Okay," I said. "So, if I'm to turn my thoughts and actions over to the care of this loving parent, what do I do?"

"I can tell you what *I* do," he said. " I use a concept of God that I took from a man named Emmet Fox—he was a New Thought spiritual leader that was followed by many in early twelve-step groups. I turn my thoughts and my actions over to the care of love, truth, life, principle, intelligence, soul, and spirit. I let these attributes guide me. I practice these aspects of a loving God and, when I waver from my course, my actions create results that I'm not happy with— I'm disciplined in this way. Try it. As a matter of fact, try the opposite. Go through a day being unloving, dishonest, without principle, and unintelligent, and see where that gets you. Ha! That's how you got here. The Big Book talks about aligning our will, or our thoughts, with God's—not His versus ours, but rather a partnership. We work together for the good of all."

I could see that what this man talked about was power, and it was easy to understand. It wasn't a way of life built on dogma, but on principle. I had no formal religious upbringing but, as I said earlier, I was Christ-based in my philosophy, and this conception didn't go against that adherence. Christ said, "Love one another; just as I have loved you…" This was a concept I could use. I altered my understanding of what God "might be" and I found power and a way out—the concept of a higher power was not the cage, it was the key.

The line "Faith without works is dead," is quoted in the Big Book. It's also a biblical line from the Book of James, and it was often used to hassle those who would talk from the side of their necks—at least that's what James used it for. At the time of that writing, there were many new Christians roaming about and they were all claiming to believe in God. "You tell me you believe in God," James said. "So what, even demons believe in God and they shudder. Show me you believe by the way you treat others." It's one of my favorite lines.

So, this is where we now stand: I've got my head around a basic understanding of "God", one which I know will expand as I grow, and I've made a decision to practice this new enlightened way of thinking…but now I need to put that decision into action. There is a prayer in the Big Book, on pg. 63; it's called the Third Step prayer.

God, I offer myself to Thee
to build with me
and to do with me as Thou wilt.
Relieve me of the bondage of self,
that I may better do Thy will.
~cont~

52

~cont~
Take away my difficulties,
that victory over them may bear witness
to those I would help of Thy Power,
Thy Love, and Thy Way of life.
May I do Thy will always!

It's a wonderful prayer—although any other prayer with the same intent will do and, as Bill wrote, "the wording *is* optional", but this is the prayer that many new people are asked to learn. I love this appeal, but I hope that when these new members are asked to learn it that they do more than just repeat the lines. I hope they're asked what these words and these lines *mean to them*. Here is how I break it down.

"God, I offer myself to Thee…"

At the word God I think of Emmet Fox's seven aspects of what "God" is: love, truth, life, principle, intelligence, soul, and spirit, and it is to these things I offer myself.

"To build with me and to do with me as Thou wilt…"

I practice those seven aspects to the best of my ability and I worry not how they might change me. At first I was afraid. I didn't want to get too good. "I'm a singer in a punk band for fuck sake. What'll this do to my ability to write and perform?" Well, I didn't have to worry about that, I definitely have not gotten "too good"—however I do show up, honor my commitments, have a strong sense

53

of community, stick my hand out to those still suffering, write more, study more, care more for people and environmental causes, and I still champion the rights of freedom and self expression. I have grown stronger by turning my life to "God". I have not grown weaker. I'm more of a threat today than I ever was, because now, I am clear, I am awake, I am principled and I am no longer a victim.

"Relieve me of the bondage of self,
that I may better do Thy will ..."

In these lines I am asking that the things which used to drive me—my plans, my scams, and my wishes, all in the interest of self—be removed, and that I'll adopt an attitude of a caring indifference to what comes, judging nothing as good or bad but seeing that it is as it is—acceptance. I will do my best to think how my actions will affect not just those around me but also all those in the world who exist with me...

"Take away my difficulties..."

Here I am not asking for the problem to be removed—that's "Magic God" business and I don't believe in the hocus pocus of fickle deities—the prayer that is the least answered is one for immortality. Many times I've been asked to pray that someone's loved-one would be saved, or live in the face of a terminal illness or horrible catastrophe; I agree to pray—and I do, but my prayer is that the family finds strength, understanding, dignity and compassion, and that they accept with love whatever outcome arises—we're all going to die. In the issue of this prayer, I'm asking that my

54

"difficulties" with my problem be removed. For example, I wouldn't ask for money; I would ask that my need for more, and my inability to live in gratitude for what I've received, be attended to. Spirituality doesn't necessarily give you more material goods, as much as it enables you to be happy with less. This applies to any illness, as well. I'm not asking to be healed and to live forever—I'm asking that I deal with my infirmary with grace, dignity, and strength. When I pray in this manner, my prayer is always answered, for in my willingness to work towards these things, and my actions in kind, they begin to be given to me or, I manifest the change. Many of us are content when we get what we want, but what if you didn't get what you want, and you were still happy.

> "That victory over them may bear witness
> to those I would help of Thy Power…"

To have victory over my difficulties is to show people how we can live in the face of what some would call adversity and pain, how we can be of service even when some would say that it was us who needed help—this is a demonstration of power. I have never received strength from someone's supposed miraculous healing, but I have definitely been inspired by the many examples of people on the program who have walked through situations that would cripple those of lesser faith. I know a woman who has been ill for as long as I've been clean. For the better part of twenty-six years I've watched her give to those around her when at times she was almost too weak to walk. I think of people like her when I recite the words victory and power.

"Thy Love, and Thy Way of life..."

Ah, the love of an understanding, unconditional, all inclusive mentor to guide and support me, and the way of life that teaches me to adopt that same conduct of love, truth, life, intelligence, soul, and spirit, and to practice them to the best of my ability in all my affairs. I think of kindness when I say this. I think of a life that's fruitful, fun, and never boring. I think of showing people how beautiful things can be, of taking them by the hand and walking them through the door of possibility and power.

"May I do Thy will always!"

Why wouldn't I want a life based on unselfish will? In the back of the Big Book there is a collection of personal stories from people who have triumphed over this illness. There is a line from one of these tales that I think of here. The story is called, "The Keys to the Kingdom."

"Now there is a sense of belonging, of being wanted and needed and loved. In return for a bottle and a hangover (and it's here I could also insert the hideous four horseman of terror, bewilderment, frustration, and despair), we've been given the Keys of the Kingdom."

You will hear many program people talk of powerlessness and how their lives are still unmanageable. Sober many years and they still claim that "people, places, and things—including alcohol," could easily get the best of them—although, there is nothing in the Big Book that backs up their beliefs. It's talk like this that stops us from

56

being useful. Could you imagine, coming to us for help and hearing a person with decades of sobriety saying that they have no more power than the newcomer? If that's the case, why stay? Why do these works?

"I'll take my chances on the street and stay the fuck out of those meetings."

Thankfully, these "powerless" members are confused (although they don't like hearing it). The first step reads, "We admitted that we *were* powerless—", meaning, that at the time they realized they were without power, they needed help—the statement is in the past tense. The step doesn't read, "We realized we are powerless—." Or "We will never have power—." It is a statement made before the work took place. The book also says that, "lack of power was our dilemma"—does that mean that even after doing the work the dilemma remains…?

"Yeah, Bill is going to write a book that says, 'Here's your dilemma, and you're still going to have it, even after you do what I tell you to do'."

Are you kidding me? Do you see how crazy that is? Those early members took these steps, and connected with a power that changed their lives; and in doing so, they were no longer powerless. If you've taken those steps and you are still "without" power, then you should go back and take them again—and please, until you do so, refrain from sharing in the meetings. People's lives depend on the clarity of your message. In the Big Book the word powerless appears only one time, and in the past tense, on pg. 59…but the word "power" appears over one hundred times. In one example:

"We have recovered and have been given the power to help others." BB pg. 132

Does that passage sound weak to you? Would you feel better if it read: "…and we've been given no power to help others—we're screwed and so are they." Come on, get off the "weak-victim" trip and let's light this up. We can go anywhere, and we can do anything when we're connected to this force. My friend Mickey B. is one of those who taught me that this program is about power. And would you like to know when this power kicks in? According to the Big Book it returns when we believe we can do it, and when we begin to live this way of life.

"As we felt new power flow in, as we enjoyed peace of mind, as we discovered we could face life successfully, as we became conscious of His presence, we began to lose our fear of today, tomorrow or the hereafter. We were reborn." BB pg. 63

…And now, let's return to that flattened ball. I was crushed, my ego deflated, the feeling of hopelessness was infused throughout my soul, but I realized that if I did what those in recovery did, practiced this way of life, that I too could recover. It was then, at that moment, that I felt new power rush in. I went from hopeless to a believer in an instant—Steps One, Two, and Three—done. I was healed from a seemingly hopeless state of mind and body, healed because I believed these steps would work; I was now willing and able to put my beliefs into action.

A Stop In Real Life

This twelve-step process takes time. There is no way around that fact. You can learn these steps, go over the basics in a few hours…but, as I said before, it takes the actual *doing* for you to really get this thing—and not just doing it once; this is a lifetime journey of experience—always growing, always changing, and hopefully, always willing to be of service. Shit, look at my conceding: I was sober almost two years before that really sank in—two years! The journey through sobriety is a series of awakenings—each one bringing you to a greater sense of awareness. Imagine, if you will, a mountain, and the higher you climb, the more you can see. But, don't be surprised if you have more "oh-shit" awakenings, than you have of those delightful "ah-ha" realizations.

When new, we are asked to establish a relationship with a loving God—one who is unconditional, inclusive, and forgiving…but, really? How can we possibly understand those attributes when we've never lived them ourselves? I knew nothing of forgiveness; I knew vindictiveness and rage. I knew nothing of unconditional love; I knew hostage taking and ownership. And, of being inclusive…all I knew was separation and detachment. It was practically impossible for me to understand a God with those positive attributes—I had no personal frame of reference from which to draw. I needed to learn how to express those qualities myself before I could really see them in another.

I have five children—three girls and two boys. The two oldest, both girls, were with me when I met my present wife; she had the

59

three youngest in tow. We're a big family now, with lots of action...but I haven't always been a great dad—I was a work in progress, and still am. The story I'm about to tell you deals with my eldest, she's twenty-seven now, but at the time she was ten, and I was nine—she used to have more sobriety than me—not any more.

I was living with my second ex-wife and I would see my eldest daughter on the weekends. I was painfully learning how to be a dad. Parenting kids can be frustrating, especially when you think *you* should be the baby: one that is catered to and always pleased...it takes hard work to sacrifice your comfort for the needs of another. Being a father doesn't entail just throwing a bit of sperm around and beating your chest—it's an exercise in learning unselfishness and service. I recommend it. Anyway, my daughter's mother came to see me one day and informed me that she was moving—I wasn't pleased. She also let me know that my daughter would be transferring to a new school. It was the middle of the school year. I think my first reaction was, "fuck you." I sought counsel—a prudent choice for men like me.

Now, I'm not going to swing into a tirade against robot-creating sponsorship here, but I will say this: if you blindly follow the orders of a sponsor, you're a stooge. However, in times of trouble, if you don't seek counsel, you're a fucking idiot. I've learned the importance of a slight pause before action. My mentor suggested that I ask my ex-wife if my daughter could stay with me so she could finish out the school year in one place. A quick note on the ex: this was a woman that I had lied to, cheated on, physically threw down with—basically made her life hell—until I began to work a program and made amends to her—look at it this way; if she hated me for the rest of her life, I couldn't fault her for it, and probably neither would

God. Surprisingly, she said, "Yes, of course she can live with you—I trust you." And if that was the only gift the twelve-step program ever gave me, it would've been enough.

My daughter moved in and we got to it. I volunteered at her school. I helped her with homework. I did my best to be a solid dad.

One afternoon my daughter was playing with a friend in our garage. I walked outside and tried the door. It was locked. I knocked.

"Baby, open up. It's Dad. What's going on?"

At first silence…and then I heard whispering and the sound of ten-year-old human rats scurrying about. "He's outside. He's at the door." They whispered. I knocked again.

"Come on, baby. Open the door. It's me. Let me in."

"Just a minute, Dad," …more scurrying and whispering. I heard a tiny voice say, "Hide that shit under the couch."

"Okay!" I yelled. "Let's go!" pounding harder. "Open the fucking door!"

"Just a minute," she said. "We'll be with you in a minute."

I was quickly getting furious—turned out by a pair of ten-year-old girls. I began to rage. "Open the fucking door. I'm feared in fifty states. Open it!"

Finally, the door was opened and the smell of cigarettes and cheap perfume assaulted me. They were smoking. I stormed in—full of rage, anger, and a moment away from violence. I was beaten when I was a child—at times harshly—and those beatings had festered into a hate that was steam-etched onto my soul. Somebody was getting the living fuck beaten out of her for this. I looked across that smoke-filled room, with eyes glazed over with rage, and there, looking back at me, was the face of a ten-year-old angel—and she

61

was terrified. When I saw that look on my little girl, I was sickened. The monster that I still could be was reflected in her eyes, and it was hideous. At that moment, I paused.

"God, please help me," I thought. "Don't let me hurt this little girl. Please."

Now, I don't know if it was "God" or my willingness to be other than what I was, but instantly, the hate and the rage and the violence was lifted from me and I looked at my little girl and I said, "I love you. Let me tell you what happened to me when I started rolling smokes."

I talked to her like one recovering alcoholic talks to another, with love and with kindness—sympathy and empathy—and then, when I was done, I told her to clean that shit up and get inside.

When I walked out I was confused. "What just happened in there? What was that?"

You see, I didn't go in there and say, "I caught you smoking so I'm going to send you to Hell, give you cancer, inflict you with AIDS, torture you, or basically, beat the living shit out of you for the rest of your life for disrespecting me!" No, I didn't say any of those things. I caught her rolling smokes and I said, "I love you."

It was then that the realization, or enlightenment, came over me: "If I'm a human being, with the smallest capacity to love, and I treated her like that, with that kindness, care, and forgiveness; and if she ever came to me, no matter what she had done, or what situation she was in, and she asked for my help, I would put my arms around her and love her with all my heart, and if I love her that much—that completely—then, how much does God love me?"

At that moment, intense warmth enveloped me—like popping a couple of Valium on a Christmas Eve—and I knew that I was

62

forgiven. I learned right then and there what it felt to truly love. That afternoon I understood that you could love someone even if his or her actions displeased you. I learned that it was okay to make mistakes, and that there was something to this life that was more than what we could touch, see, or taste. That afternoon I took a few steps toward a greater understanding of those positive attributes, and I began to climb above what I had been.

"There is nothing noble in being superior to your fellow man; true nobility is being superior to your former self."

Ernest Hemingway

The "We…"

Before we continue let's discuss the wording of these steps—especially regarding the plurality.

A lot is said about the "We" of the program and how, "We" do nothing alone; but the "We" was used as narrative to explain what the first "group" of drunks did to recover. Bill isn't saying that they took each step as a collective—simultaneously—he's saying that *as a group* they individually took these steps. Imagine it as a high-school reunion of sorts, the classes of 1935 to 1939 said, "We attended Bill W. High School."

I guarantee that one-day, or one late night, you will be alone, and all that will stand between you and destruction is whatever you have inside. You're the one that must look within; *we* can't do it for you. We can guide you, and share the path *we* took, but we can't go inside your mind or heart and tell you where you stand…it's up to *you* as an individual to take these actions yourself. But, if it's any consolation, when you do take these steps, you too will be able to say, "Here's what "*We*" did…"

A Quick Note From Me To You

This next section was a pain in the ass to write. It's easier to take a fourth step than it is to explain it. I've gone through this step many times—taking my own inventory, and helping others with theirs, but this is the first time that I've ever tried to convey the process through written words—not sitting chair to chair over a cup of coffee, communicating with a language that could never be put to page, and I'm realizing how hard it is to explain a process that has taken me twenty-six years to uncover, a process whose pathway to understanding is always changing, almost like playing a complicated child's game with no rules.

"Move here." I tell you. "Stop. Now, move there. Think of what that means to you. Let it sink in. Okay, now turn around, go back to where you just were and start over. Dance for a moment. Great, now move forward and see how different it is…"

At each stop of our journey our understanding grows—we change, we become a new creation, and we're stepping away from the "alcoholic mind" and entering into greater awareness. Doing this step is not just putting pen to paper, as many of us have been told—doing this step is really about becoming aware of ourselves, our purpose, and seeing ourselves as others see us, and, I want you to know it can take years.

The alcoholic practically has the market cornered on self-centeredness. Our perception is always from the inside out: "Look at what they're doing," we say, "How can they be so inconsiderate?" Gradually, as we begin to awake, we start to see ourselves as others see us—these steps can generate that change in perspective. There was an elder in our group—the honcho if you will, Frank H, a man whom people admired, and indeed the majority of our members hung on his words with reverence. He was a great man, kind, loving and all-inclusive. He was a man with power. One morning, during his pitch, he told the group that they didn't need to worry about working the steps. "They'll work you," he said. I was infuriated. At the time, I was a driven, strictly-by-the-book member of the program. Here was his chance to tell those people to "read, study, and dive in like your life depended on it"…and instead, he told them not to bother. Shit—it took me a while to fully understand why he said that. He wasn't telling people not to take the steps; he was telling them that there is an awakening that can't be forced. It appears like a surprise summer rain to the parched coastal valleys. That, if you stop drinking, there might come a day when your head will clear, a day when you inadvertently walk before a mirror, and instead of a quick casual glance at a stranger, you see yourself for what you really are. Your fourth step is written in your eyes, and you know what you need to do—you admit where you've fallen short and you set out to reconcile.

I'm going to break down this step into two parts: the uncovering and connecting to the power aspect (i.e., the theory), and then the practical (i.e., the basic inventory). If it's confusing, call me. My number is 714-969-9835. We could have a cup of coffee and I'll straighten you out.

68

Uncovering The Power

In a previous chapter this phrase was mentioned: "lack of power, was our dilemma." It's from the Big Book, pg. 45, and, to a point, that statement is correct...but is it really power that we are without, or, is the dilemma instead our *inability* to access the power within us?

When I first entered the program I was dismayed. In the meetings it was suggested that I was powerless and that I would remain so until I died—probably from the effects of alcoholism—and yet, I was told that I could connect to a power that could save me, a power greater than myself.

"Connect...so just where is this power cord located and how much cable do I need to string it to heaven?"

It's at this point in the journey that I beg you, please seek guidance from someone who does more than just repeat phrases that they heard in a meeting—and when you receive that guidance, don't accept it on face value alone, but also study the concepts for yourself and do your own research. I discovered that I was not doomed to be powerless for all time, and the connection that I needed to plug into was no further than inside me. On pg. 55 of the Big Book, Bill mentions a "God" consciousness that resides in us all, and, in the appendix to the spiritual experience, he goes on to explain that our members tapped an *"unsuspected inner resource which they presently identify with their own conception of a Power greater than themselves"*—a "God" within.

"Well," you might ask yourself, "if the power is within, why have I been so without?"

Have you ever forgotten to plug in an appliance, missed a switch, or installed something improperly? Have the battery cables on your car ever become loose or corroded? These disconnections to power are similar to what we're currently dealing with. The "Kingdom of God" might reside within, but we're unable to access its existence because between us and it, lays an ego fueled by selfishness and pride—a corrosion of fear-based character defects that hinder our connection. And this is the purpose of that fourth step, to chart the obstructions in the channel, to help us become aware of why we've failed to connect.

"But I've felt good before. I've felt empowered. I've gone through stretches where I've accomplished many things."

Yeah, I get it. I questioned this myself. I've also accomplished things, and at moments I'd felt empowered…but why didn't it last? There were times that I attempted to adopt a healthier philosophy. I'd eat right, do yoga, and pray. I was a born-again Christian for a few weeks…of course, that's because I was trying to sleep with a girl who was also "saved"—"Yeah, I love Jesus too sweetheart"—but that's another story. I'd often read spiritual books and at times listened to talks from "enlightened" teachers. And when I did, I felt pretty good…for a while, and then the "good news" began to wear on me, and then, wear off. I'd drift away, becoming dissatisfied and discontent, until I wandered into the next new thing that I thought would fix me. The majority of these spiritual works or ideas were wonderful, containing useful information that's been passed around for centuries—those that adopt them do benefit from their use, but I never put positive thought to action. I listened. I enjoyed the idea

70

of it, but spiritually I was like a stagnant pond. You could fill my heart and my head with the clear water of love, and I'd be invigorated and vibrant, but then that beautiful energy would soon become stale and useless—it would stagnate and fester. For water to stay healthy it must flow, and the spirit is no different: in order to be useful, vital, and strong that spirit must move through us—a Mobius strip of never-ending power.

I'm sure you've been asked if you see the glass as half-empty or half-full, but trip with me for a moment and picture it as neither…rather, envision the glass as a vessel for an essence that is moving, abundant, and never ending—as long as we share it with others. When I reach out to you, the power that resides in me—but which has lain dormant—connects with the power that resides in you, and God, or Higher Power, or an Inner Resource, appears in the midst. It's as if an invisible cable connects these human terminals—we touch, we spark.

There's a wonderful Christ quote, which supports this philosophy:

"Where two or three are assembled in my name, there I am in the midst."

When you look at the phrase, "in my name", ask yourselves, what is he really saying? When we say those words what we're usually inferring is, "This is what this person stands for"; in Christ's case, he stood for love, kindness, inclusivity, and unlimited power. So, by reaching out to another, in the spirit of love and service…this force appears. The best part is, especially for you Hindus, Muslims, Jews, Wiccans, Buddhists, agnostics, atheists, etc.…you don't have to believe in Christ to achieve these same results—you can believe in anything, or nothing, just reach out to those around you. The combination of one connecting to another through love and service manifests power—the "God" within appears.

"I love you, my brother, whoever you are - whether you worship in a church, kneel in your temple, or pray in your mosque. You and I are children of one faith, for the diverse paths of religion are fingers of the loving hand of the one supreme being, a hand extended to all, offering completeness of spirit to all, eager to receive all."
Khalil Gibran

Baking A Cake

Albert was hungry. He wanted cake—a nice, moist, white cake like his mother used to bake. He went to the market and cruised the cake aisle. There on the top row, above all other boxes of easy-bake cake, was the one he wanted. Betty Crocker, that was the brand he'd been served it as a child. The picture looked marvelous. It was a spongy, taste-satisfying, delectable item begging Albert to take it home. He did. He brought the box into his kitchen and he reverently opened it. He poured the contents into a bowl. He added eggs, water and oil, and then he mixed it as directed. Albert greased a pan, poured the batter in, and he popped it in a pre-heated oven. That evening Albert enjoyed a delicious slice of his traditional white cake.

That same evening Evelyn was at the market. She also was hungry but she didn't know what for. She'd been served many things, but tonight, none of them sounded satisfying. She walked past the bargain rack. There were many boxes there, the majority of which had lost their labels. She reached for one of the containers. It's exterior was an inconspicuous brown cardboard. She had no idea what it held. Evelyn took the box home. She carried it almost carelessly into the kitchen and she opened it. There were instructions. She grabbed a bowl, poured the contents in, added eggs, water, and oil, and then she mixed it as directed. She poured the batter into a greased pan and she popped it in a pre-heated oven. In less than an hour Evelyn enjoyed a very moist and spongy slice of white cake.

Albert was a believer. He had an image in his mind that he'd had since childhood. It was as it always had been. Some of us have an image of God in our minds, an image we constructed, or was given to us, when we were children. Others, like Evelyn, aren't sure where they're going or who, if anyone, will appear when they get there. They might have been raised agnostic or even as an atheist. My conception of God changes with each breath I take. The image I brought to the program dissolved long ago. I have friends that are Christians and friends that are Jews. I have friends that are agnostic and those that are atheists. All of us are sober. We followed the same directions, working with the same materials of flesh and spirit—our beliefs were not uniform, but our outcome is.

The Power Continued

"Okay, I understand that I need to chart the obstructions in the way, clear the channel between this force and myself so I can access this power…but why? Can't I access this strength and still be an asshole? What do my character defects have to do with tapping into what's inside of me—it's my God—isn't it?"

Yes, it is your God, but the philosophy of twelve-step living is basically one of service. The way to continually access and utilize this power is to channel it through unselfish actions—one alcoholic working with another. In other words, altruism: a word for the principle of selflessness, empathy, and having a strong regard for the welfare of others. In my case, it entailed taking those spiritual teachings that I'd enjoyed and actually applying them in real life. As Bill writes on pg. 44, "To be doomed to an alcoholic death or to live on a spiritual basis are not always easy alternatives to face."

"So you're saying that for me to have power I need to serve? Are you kidding? I've been a servant to alcohol and drugs for most of my life, and now you're saying I get a new master?"

Yeah, I wasn't happy about it either, but sometimes, through study, you will find ideas that don't align with what you already believe. Instead, these concepts challenge you to think along new directions. It also helps to have your ass thoroughly beaten and your roadmap of "how to get by in this world" burned to ashes— "sweetly reasonable," my old man used to call it—when you're so beat down that you're willing to take suggestions—or, live life on a spiritual basis.

On pg. 62 of the Big Book, Bill also writes, "We must be rid of self or it will kill us." Now, if we accept that statement as a truth, then those words function as a sort of primer for the rest of the steps: a principle, or code of conduct if you will, one that demands we forego self-seeking; so we need to examine carefully our upcoming work based on that code. That being said, we take none of these steps for ourselves; we take them to benefit others, or, to be better servants to those around us. Here are a few examples of this principle from the Big Book:

Pg. 20 "Our very lives, as ex-problem drinkers, depend upon our constant thought of others and how we may help meet their needs."

Pg. 77 "Our real purpose is to fit ourselves to be of maximum service to God and the people about us."

Pgs. 14-15, "For if an alcoholic failed to perfect and enlarge his spiritual life through work and self-sacrifice for others, he could not survive the certain trials and low spots ahead."

So, there within the pages of that big book, lie the answers to why we do an inventory—which are ultimately reasons beyond just staying sober. We are meant to be servants, and the power gained is not solely for "us", but for "them"; however, don't be too discouraged by the demands of this process—as discussed in a previous section, by serving them we all ultimately benefit. This is known as "enlightened self-interest", or, to take things a step

76

further, "servant leadership". We use the channel of service to create our flow. We take the God within and direct it to helping others, and in doing so, the channel of power is open and the force flows through, keeping us sober, enriching our lives, and giving us a meaning and purpose to live.

"Okay, so our very lives depend on us being helpful and channeling that power...but what if our character defects make us so unattractive that no one would want our help—or, what if we're just too lazy or afraid to get off our asses and affect change?"

Bingo! That's what I'm talking about. If power flows from me to you and I'm such an insufferable asshole that you don't want my help, then wham—I die—probably after another horrific bender.

Let's pretend that we have a problem, an embarrassing situation that's been troubling us, something we wouldn't want the neighbors to know about, and for which we've decided to seek help or counsel. In a situation like this, whom would we turn to: someone who is closed-minded, judgmental, or unwilling to share his or her time with us? Of course not, as a matter of fact we would search out the exact opposite; we would look for someone who has an understanding nature, who is non-judgmental and willing to listen. *This* is why we do an inventory: not to just stay sober—which is a move based on self, but to find the defects in our character that render us useless or unattractive to those seeking assistance.

The Nuts and Bolts

There are many methods of conducting an inventory. Bill writes, before his example on pg. 65, that "we were usually as definite as this example", meaning, not always, sometimes we do it other ways; he then goes on to use lines and columns to illustrate *his* method. However, one of the co-founders of twelve-step recovery, Dr. Bob, used an entirely different device. In one example, in the story "He Sold Himself Short," Dr. Bob listened as the alcoholic Earl T. related his "story"…and then the doctor "inventoried" him, and supplied Earl with a list of his character defects!

Ouch—I've tried that method before, and I wasn't pleased with the results.

"I do what?" I said.

"Yes," was the reply, "you do that daily; and it's fucking annoying."

So if we look at these two inventories, the main difference—other than style—is that Bill focuses mainly on our resentments, fears, and sexual nature, while Bob's inventory touches on a few of the more sophisticated defects like sarcasm, jealousy, and intolerance. What I'm going to show you here will be a mixture of the two, and I've found this combination very useful. It's important to list our resentments, as Bill did, and it's necessary to acknowledge our fears and our sexual misconduct—but it's also a valuable tool to look at specific defects of character and how they factor in our lack of usefulness to others. I'm going to begin with Bill's "big three" and then I'll jump into a few variations of the seven deadly sins…

"Whoa, slow up Jack. You're not going to go all medieval on us...are you?"

"No, I'm not going to break out the hot oil, the iron maiden and the pinchers...but as character defects go, the seven deadlies are pretty solid indicators of poor behavior."

Resentment

The first time I listed my resentments I let 'em fly, page after page of "those mother-fuckers" and what they'd done to me—I was a victim extraordinaire. That is, until Bill suggested that I look back and see where and how I had placed myself in a position to be hurt. Every one of my resentments could be traced back to an action I had taken—a selfish move on my part that set the train of reprisal rolling, with me jumping headlong under its wheels. Have you ever heard the story of the alcoholic who killed his parents? He was arrested for the crime and when he came before the bench he asked the judge for leniency, "You see sir, I'm an orphan." I'll tell you, there's a certain smug satisfaction you get when you can blame your problems on others, and the sympathy you can generate as you relate your tale of woe is practically unending—but where does it get you? It got me nowhere. Until I was willing to take full responsibility I was weak, without power, and my life would never get better unless the offending assholes begged my forgiveness and changed their ways. If they're the problem I'm screwed, but if I'm the problem, if my perception of the situation can be altered, then the power shifts to me. I never realized how much strength there is in the statement,

"It's my fault." As I mentioned earlier, there are situations where we could easily play the victim, e.g., issues of child abuse, molestation, rape, etc., and believe me, you can readily get people to cosign on your right to stay hurt, your right to lead a life of pain and despair…but is that really what you want? If that's the case, consider yourself a co-conspirator in the crime perpetrated against you. How exactly does our victimhood make us useful to those around us? Ask yourself—how long *can you* tolerate a victim? Not to be a prick or anything, but after I hear the same tale of woe a hundred times over, I feel like kicking the victim's ass. So, we list our resentments and then we see how we placed ourselves in a position to be hurt, or allowed what was done to us to fester and make us weak. We change our perception of the problem and then, to make ourselves useful we become willing to use our experience in a positive way to help others step away from *their* anger and *their* hurt.

Here's a side note on the real dangers of victimhood and resentment. The bottom line is, as alcoholics, if we drink we die— either physically or spiritually via our disconnection to others. Playing the continual victim is a position that leads us into the "poor me's" of alcoholism, the "Look how badly I've been treated, it's no wonder I'm such a failure" stand that needs a little nerve-relaxer to soothe. I hate to say it but, "poor me, poor me, pour me another drink." As for resentment, other than needing a cocktail to relieve that angry tension, have you ever driven while angry? Were you a stickler for the "rules of the road", making sure that your parking job was a between-the-lines beauty that left space for those around? If you were like me, when I was angry I thought of nothing other than what they'd done to me. I used my car as a weapon and I parked head-in, five feet from the curb, and "fuck-em" if they didn't

81

like it. Resentment cuts us off from the "sunlight of the spirit"; in other words, when I'm resentful I revert back to that self-centered baby unaware of my surroundings and my relationship to the world. And, when I'm angry, full of hate, and I'm offered a drink, do you really think I'm capable of pausing and thinking where this drink will lead me? No. I reach without thought, ingest without restraint.

There was an old man named George D, he was sober forty years, and he was a friend. He said he liked me because I read loud and I was full of life. I think he liked watching me get myself into trouble and try to get out. One day George came to me with a question.

"Jack," he said, in a voice gravelly from age and booze. "Remember that we deal with alcohol: cunning, baffling and powerful…what's the keyword there, young man?"

I thought for a moment. "It's cunning, George—a real sneaky little illness."

"No," he said. "I like where you're coming from but that's not it."

"I knew it wasn't," I returned. "It's baffling. Look at me. I'm totally clueless."

"Yes, you are clueless Son, but that's not what I'm looking for."

"Ha!" I said. "I knew it wasn't. I was playing with you, man. It's powerful. Powerful business we got up in here, George."

"Nope," he said. "That's not it either."

"Hold up, Gramps. That's all three, man."

"It's remember," he said. "*Remember* we deal with alcohol…remember, remember, remember!"

Shit, I can't tell you how many times I forgot. Resentment took me out of my awareness. Victimhood gave me an excuse to be loaded.

Fear

Fear is a word that's saved my ass but has also rendered me useless. Some would say that we should be completely without it—live courageously at all times. Yeah, those same people also haven't read about the link between fear and the area of our brain that controls basic impulse control and decision-making (e.g., fear keeps me from grabbing Mrs. Johnson's ass in the market); when it comes to self-control, a touch of fear helps us make wise decisions. But that's not what I'm talking about here. I'm referring to those fears that hinder us from living a successful, happy life…fears that trap us like frightened animals within ourselves. Once again, look at the fears that stop you from being useful, that keep you from connecting. I've struggled with a fear of flying. At times, it's a real bitch. It's kept me from doing things I love—visiting places that I'd like to see. I was invited to speak in the New Orleans area a short time after hurricane Katrina had hit. I was afraid to get on a plane. I didn't go. At the time I had a friend who was in Louisiana helping with insurance claims. I told him what I'd done.

"You know, Jack," he said. "We were hit really hard down here. The place is in ruins and we're doing our best to recover. We sure could have used you—it would've been nice to laugh."

My fear rendered me useless. Today I fly quite a bit and I've got a trick that works fairly well. On the plane I turn my attention to those around me—especially, those that might find flying uncomfortable. I talk to them, smile, and try to ease their pain. It helps—all of us.

"Fear is the main source of superstition, and one of the main sources of cruelty. To conquer fear is the beginning of wisdom." Bertrand Russell

Sexual Misconduct

God bless Bill on this one. In the Big Book he isn't concerned with "who we do" or "what we do" as long as we do it unselfishly. How's that for progressive? In the end, that's the bottom line: Are you a selfish, uncaring, dishonest lover—seeking only the fulfillment of your needs...or are you not? Some prudish program people have said that our sexual activities can get us loaded but who are they to judge? In the Big Book, Bill says that there are some that cry for "more" and others that cry for "less". Personally, I don't care what anyone does or who they're with; however, if you're continually using people selfishly, the chances of you getting loaded are probably pretty high—and not because you're having sex, but because a person who selfishly uses others has probably not had the necessary spiritual awakening to stay sober—they're still wrapped up in getting "their's". My sexual conduct was not always one of unselfishness. I lied. I cheated. I did things I wasn't proud of—and that was in sobriety. I think the moment that really brought me into

84

awareness of this defect was when I heard a piece of gossip. There was a man struggling with his alcoholism—he couldn't get a hold on the program. It was suggested that he come to me—his reply, "Why would I go to him? He can't even keep his dick in his pants." There it was, my behavior—this time in regards to my sexual conduct—had again rendered me useless. Bill W. suggests that if you struggle with your sexual impulses, you should turn that energy towards helping others—it's much less damaging. Today, I practice unselfishness in my relationship, and my wife and I get to practice...well, basically, whatever we want.

Pride

There are many ways to look at this defect, but here we're going to dissect pride as it might manifest itself in terms of a hindrance to service. Wisdom and intelligence are characteristics you would want to find in a guide or confidant, but what if we've "seen it all, and done it all"? With an attitude like this we close ourselves off to new experiences and teachings. Do you listen to and read information to be challenged, or are you searching for words and passages that support your own entrenched point of view? Are you willing to step outside your comfort zone and see where a person with a completely different perspective and set of principles might be right, and are you willing to let yourself entertain, or be challenged by, their beliefs? I once heard a man in a meeting say, "The ripe fruit rots on the vine." If that is so, when we're satisfied with the limited knowledge that we've acquired, and we're no longer willing to grow,

85

then we cease being useful. The more we can learn, the more valuable is our connection—as long as we remember that what we know as truth today could quite possibly become tomorrow's lie.

"Can you give us an example of pride in our meetings?"

"Yeah, sure. Fuck Hector. He always has his hand up and he shares the same shit everyday. I'm a second away from throwing my poorly-brewed cup of coffee on him."

"Come on, Jack. How does that help?"

"It helps like this…"

Are you accepting of another's lifestyle and journey, or do you hold to a certain code to which you feel others should also subscribe? Tolerance is a virtue that we can't do without. To realize the freedom inherent in each individual and to celebrate the landscape of colors that is humanity—that acceptance is a true representation of being spiritual. When I was new, a man walked past me at a meeting, smiled and said, "We need you here, just as you are." I told him to fuck off. I thought he was making fun of me, smart-assing my green hair and pajama pants, but he wasn't. He stopped to tell me that he was serious; that the strength of a twelve-step program is not in the common bond that holds us together—our recovery from alcoholism—but in our *individuality*. Our different experiences and lifestyles are such that one of us, one member in the group, could quite possibly have something randomly in common with a new person seeking assistance…something that others of us don't have and by sharing it, help that new person identify their illness. The greater our diversity the stronger we become as a collective toolkit—not one wrench, or set of ideas to fit any situation, but many, a legion of connections waiting to be deployed.

I find it interesting that so many hardcore twelve-step people scream about the "164" (for those of you unfamiliar, some members consider those pages to be the real "program" part of the Big Book—the most important, the rest I guess is filler); but when they tout the "164" they're leaving out the Dr.'s opinion, Dr. Bob's story, the Twelve Traditions, the spiritual experience, and most importantly, the personal accounts in the back of the book. Bill once wrote that the heart of the program lay in our personal stories, and if so, those who scream for the "164" are screaming for a cadaver with no heart. So, when we're examining Pride, we want to look at where we have been close-minded, judgmental, and intolerant. List those behaviors and move on.

As for Hector, the next time he shares, I'm going to listen with not just my head but also my heart. I'm going to hear what he says, feel his words, and meditate on why that message is so important to him.

Greed

Greed isn't always about money—that's actually the basest form of this defect. Greed, in our case, is an unwillingness to give of our time and share ourselves. Dropping a dollar in the collection basket at a meeting or donating to a charity is noble, but to sit with another and to connect is channeling the divine. Do you spend time with the newcomer, listen as they speak, or expose a part of you that might be embarrassing or uncomfortable? Do you reach out to old-timers? Yeah, a lot of them have been sober for decades but that doesn't exclude them from loneliness or depression. When we share our time we can help others establish connections that alleviate pain and leave a lasting impression. Sometimes your kind word or a moment or two of companionship can turn the tide of depression. I know of many times when a simple text sent my way brightened my day.

One of my favorite scenes from Dickens' *A Christmas Carol*, is when Scrooge faces the ghost of his old partner Jacob Marley who is trapped in a wandering, existential limbo, covered in the heavy chains that symbolize the prison he forged in his earlier, money-obsessed life.

"But you were always a good man of business, Jacob," faltered Scrooge, who now began to apply this to himself.

"Business!" cried the ghost, wringing its hands again. "Mankind was my business. The common welfare was my business; charity, mercy, forbearance, and benevolence, were, *all*, my business. The dealings of my trade were but a drop of water in the comprehensive ocean of my business!"

Ah, poor Marley, he discovered his purpose too late. An inventory taken after death does the ghost no good.

Sloth

To exhibit unwillingness; lack of action, and to rest on our laurels. How hard is it to get off your ass and get moving, start writing an inventory, call a sponsor or mentor, or just do something as simple as a morning meditation or prayer? I used to hear people talk about the "10,000-pound phone" and it drove me crazy. "The phone weighs nothing," I thought, "it's the mind that adds the weight." Yeah, it's the mind all right, and I've struggled with it as much as anyone. Establishing a simple daily discipline can combat this, but you must *do* it; and it doesn't have to be a grand action, a whole carnival of "getting shit done"…one slight move a day can get you rolling. (That is, if you can get your ass away from social media)!

If we're taking inventory of where we've been slothful, let's look around and see what has yet to be done; then, if you get around to finishing that, ask yourself, "Why don't I want the gifts that action would bring?" Sometimes, a trip back to the old alcoholic furnace can be a great motivator when we're slow to move.

Envy

Gossip, and shit talking, I've never met anyone who likes to dish out more dirt than an alcoholic. One of my friends—now deceased, used to start his chatter by saying, "What do you got for me?" He was constantly looking for dirt and, sadly, there were times that I supplied. I didn't give out any "vaulted" secrets, but I wasn't against passing on a couple of the latest juicy tidbits. I guess I really don't need to expand on how this can hurt someone, but in a program where the members' very lives depend on love, tolerance, and connection, and you drive someone away by creating strife and embarrassment…well, the cost of a few careless words can indeed mean death. Take a moment to truly understand that we're dealing with human lives here—and don't buy into the bullshit that you can't make someone "go out". I know that no one can make you feel bad without your consent, but we're not dealing with strong people, especially when they're new. Loneliness, despair and disconnection, brought about by your words, can lead someone right back to the bottle.

"It was said long ago that there were three classes of people in the world, and while they are subject to variation, for elemental consideration they are useful. The first is that large class of people who talk about people; the next class is comprised of those who talk about things; and in the third class are those who discuss ideas. All of us are conscious of this and we have also realized how distasteful the lower thought is after we have accustomed ourselves to the higher." Origin of Mental Species by Henry James Derbyshire

Lust

I've already touched on sexual misconduct, but this 'deadly sin' is different. This is that leering, lip-smacking "pervo" that makes your skin feel greasy. Lusting after your significant other is healthy and it's fun, but lusting after strangers, or non-strangers who don't welcome your advances is downright invasive. If you're a woman, I'm sure you've run into a couple of inappropriate huggers—those creepy bastards you can't shake loose. Hell, I'm a big guy and I've had the reach-around-butt-lift-grab-hug inflicted on me a few times—the women can be just as predatory as the men. Look, a quick flirty glance is okay, but if it's not returned, stop it. Check yourself; ask a friend if you're not sure if you're that Peter Lore type, all bug-eyed and drooling. Be complimentary; by all means, tell someone that they look nice, that their top looks good with their eyes, but creepy…no. And for you macho homophobic men, practice telling other guys that they look good, it's a blast. I told someone that I really liked his slacks and that his shirt looked great with his eyes—it

90

basically froze him in his tracks and had him blushing like a sissy violet.

Gluttony

Like greed, gluttony doesn't necessarily have to do with just overeating as much as it has to do with overdoing anything. There are many of us who stop ingesting the booze and then start ingesting anything that'll fill that "God" sized hole in our soul. I've overdone it all: smoking, gambling, eating, sexing, and basically anything that felt good. If it's worth doing, it's most surely worth doing to excess. It's "all good" in its just measure, but temperance and balance are the key words here. When inventorying this defect look for the pursuits that take you away from being of service, that rob you of the time that should be spent with others. And, when you're looking at what takes you away from service, don't forget to look at the time you spend in meetings or program pursuits. There are many who hide in twelve-step groups, "giving" of themselves, and yet saving nothing for those people they have at home: their families.

I had a sponsor who came down with incurable lung cancer. I'd visit him in the hospital, and at his home when he was about to die. One evening, I was set to bring him a snack and chat by his bed, but as I was heading out of the house my youngest daughter said, "Are you leaving again?" It was heartbreaking. I got sober so this little girl wouldn't have to hurt, and now, I was hurting her with my "I'm Mr. twelve-step" personality—"the poster boy of sobriety". I wasn't going anywhere. I called my sponsor on the phone and told him what happened. I said I'd bring him a cup of coffee in the morning. I could almost feel him smile across the phone line.

"Jack," he said. "If you would've left that little girl to come see me…then I would have failed with you."

It was the last thing he said to me. He died the next day.

People will tell you that sobriety is the most important, and yes, if I'm loaded I have nothing—but sobriety by itself is not enough— "The elimination of drinking is but a beginning. A much more important demonstration of our principles lies before us in our respective homes, occupations and affairs." BB Pg. 19. My friend Pete used to say that sobriety was first among equals, meaning when he was with his wife and family they were most important; when he was at work, the job took that spot—giving his all to the company; and when he was called to be of service to the program, that became number one—all things important under the sober umbrella of recovery.

Wrath

Wrath is a strange one. It sits hand-in-hand with resentment, but it goes much further: wrath steps into punishment, payback, and false pride. Wrath is the action of one who refuses to look within, who finds their behaviors to reside above others'…to be less offensive. I often think that desire is at times clothed in wrath, that we secretly envy those who've upset us; we wish we could get away with being such cunts. I was a vindictive prick. I was hurt, so you should be too. When someone crossed the line I considered my payback as "free-game," as if it was almost my duty, to deliver his or her sentence. I was full of the hate that generated the wrath.

There's a great Bible story that fits nicely here—it's the one when the elders are going to stone the adulterous woman. They've got their rocks, and they've got their anger, and they have their sense of duty and pride. The first stone is about to be cast and then Christ rolls up. He sits on the ground and writes with his finger in the dust.

"Let he without sin throw the first stone."

That's when I crowd to the front and say, "Give me a rock. I'll bag that nasty old tramp in the head!"

Yes, self-centered and selfish to the extreme, I'm a great judge of your actions, and my skill as an accuser and a punisher is legendary...but I couldn't see myself. I came to this program as a liar, a cheat, an adulterer, a thief, and an anarchistic bomb maker...and I had the nerve to get angry with you because you didn't have the coffee done on time. It's amazing I'm still alive. What Christ did was to ask the elders to look at themselves and to see beyond the degrees of sin—see the fact that we have all, in some way, transgressed. Bill W. asks us to view those who have harmed us as "sick" men, and when doing so, we're able to separate the man from the actions. We all have varying degrees of mental illness. We act out of fear and not always in a healthy way. My friend Frank used to say, "If they knew better, they'd do better"...that is, if they were capable of it. I ask you to look at yourselves, to inventory where you have transgressed and to be willing to right those wrongs—if *you* are capable of seeing it. I've heard it said that if you don't take an inventory, you're sure to drink again, and that could be true, but is that really the punishment for not putting pen to paper, or is it just not waking up?

"Your visions will become clear only when you can look into your own heart. Who looks outside, dreams; who looks inside, awakes."

C.G. Jung

Confession

Confession can be a frightening word—to stand tall, or maybe with head bowed and admit our wrongdoings to another. Yes, if I was confessing to one who had never transgressed, I might be a touch hesitant at laying my deeds before that person's feet. Thankfully, in program, we're confessing to fallen women and disgraced men—a rogue's gallery of reformed ne'er-do-wells who've sullied as much ground as we've walked upon. My favorite confessor was a cleaned up ex-junkie barber who matched me sin for sin.

"You know Bob," I said, "I might've fooled around with the dog a bit..." He smiled before he replied.

"Was he a collie?"

Relax; I'm playing with you, but the fact that we're talking to those not lily-white does make confessing easier. But what are we confessing really? We're looking for the defect not the story. Our confessor is not there to make judgment, only to help us see ourselves as we are. In that case, who better to talk to than those who have failed, or fallen short before us? I've heard some say that you could give your inventory to a deaf mute but how would that serve you? The Big Book suggests that we read our inventory to one who is able to keep a confidence and would fully understand what we're driving at—meaning, they're familiar with the journey into the world of the spirit and they realize that just admitting where we've fallen short is not enough for us...we're going to make right of our wrongs.

Speaking as someone who has been the confessor, there is honor and responsibility in hearing confession—my friends and I call it "being in the vault," or in jest, "the cone of silence." It's an understanding between us that this conversation is not to be shared, nor treated lightly. Hearing confession is sacred. I've been on the other end of a less-than-closed-mouth confessor, and I was not pleased. We were talking before a meeting and I had just confessed to being unfaithful to an ex, when a man approached us. He asked how we were doing and my confessor told him, "I'm just trying to talk him into being faithful to his girl." It was horrifying, and the last time I ever told that man anything. I choose my confidants with prudence now—and, I practice monogamy. That being said, pick wisely who you're going to share with, and it does not have to be your "sponsor". There's an old-timer in our area that got sober in the '60s. He was part of a group that read their inventories to the same man—one of their members had found a hip, spiritually-based therapist who understood, so the group chose him to be their confessor and they lined up. The last time I checked this old-timer was still sober, still active, and very vibrant, so I guessed it worked out well.

I've found that once you find someone you can trust, and who understands, you'll probably find it easy to reveal yourself—if anything, sometimes we reveal too much. I once had a man tell me to stop.

"Jack" he said, "I don't need to hear another goddamn example of you being abusive and unfaithful in your relationships. I get it. The first six established the pattern, now you're just wasting time."

On the flipside of that, another thing I've found important is: don't let your partner be too soft on you—co-sign off on your bullshit. We need to be hit hard, fully shaken, and come clear about

96

where we've fallen short of the mark. This is not a step to be taken lightly.

A note to those hearing confession: help your penitent dig and be clear, but watch for those who want to beat themselves up. Remind them that they were mentally ill, and that while we take responsibility for our actions, we are not what we did. That being said; let them hurt a bit—let it sink in that we were quite the little shits while drinking and that what we did harmed others...at times gravely. The ego is a resilient beast and at this juncture it needs to be ridden hard and hopefully put away tear-stained and wet.

As for feeling connected after taking this step—as the Big Book implies—that wasn't my experience. I was happy to get it done, and I felt like I was part of the group, but ego deflation never feels good to me. I can't say that I was walking hand in hand on the "broad spiritual highway," as the book implies. I wasn't what I thought I was, and it shook me pretty hard. I was rocketed into a reality of what it was to be human. Ugh.

So, be clear: be thorough, do your best to trust, and let the movie roll through to the credits. After all, it's just your whole life being played unabashedly before you so enjoy it. Sometimes the harsh light of reality hurts, but the glare of that awakening can lead us into a harmonious state of love.

At times I've wondered, what is the necessity of bringing someone else into this confession? I've admitted my transgressions to God and to myself; do we really need another dick on the dance floor?

I've confessed to being heavily agnostic in my beliefs, and so, if I admit to God I'm admitting to more of an ideal than an entity, and there's no real connection in that act. When I sit before another person and bare myself—holding nothing back—I avail myself completely to the spirit that courses through humanity. I am neither hindered nor obstructed by ego. At that moment I am connected and I am whole.

"I am personally convinced that the basic search of every human being, from the cradle to the grave, is to find at least one other human being before whom he can stand completely naked, stripped of all pretense or defense, and trust that person not to hurt him, because that other person has stripped himself naked, too."
Alan McGinnis

Resist not Evil

I was tempted to write, "resist not ego" but, one time I pulled that shit in a meeting and I was called up short. I'd heard someone exchange the word "evil" with the word "ego" in the "Lord's prayer"—"Deliver me from ego" they said. I thought it was extremely witty. I adopted it for about two meetings. I was standing next to an old-timer and thought, here we go—I'll thrill him with this.

"And deliver me from ego," I said.

Afterward, this older member approached me, "How much ego does it take to change a 2,000-year-old prayer?" I never said it again.

As for Steps Six and Seven in the Big Book, they are covered by two paragraphs—one paragraph being a prayer—it's perfect.

I know that Bill later expanded these—and our membership will spend days chattering about their defects of character, but what if he had it right all along and they needed no expansion? There is a principle that is called, "resist not evil," and it is the belief that when we fight something, we give power to that which we fight. This principle has always been one of my favorites. I was raised in the '60s, alive when Dr. Martin Luther King. Jr. was assassinated, and to "resist not evil" was a principle he lived by.

"Returning hate for hate multiplies hate, adding deeper darkness to a night already devoid of stars. Darkness cannot drive out darkness; only light can do that." Dr. M.L.K., Jr.

So, what is the evil that we shouldn't resist? Are we talking about some red-cloaked, horned man who lurks beneath the stairs? Of course not, this is not fantasy, this is reality. I'm more a believer in the Satan of Judaism: the *yetzer hara,* or the inclination to serve one's own selfish needs instead of the good of God or all. There are also three Greek words for evil that fit well here: *kakos,* which is basically chaos against order; *poneros,* which is that which causes pain and suffering; and *phaulos,* which is stupid, foolish, unwise, or thoughtless. If we combine these, what do we have? The traits of a selfish, self-centered alcoholic who has created his own misery by letting his fears and irrational wants drive him to destruction. These defects of character are what we are going to stop resisting.

In the Big Book, Bill asks if we're ready to have these defects removed. Are you kidding? Look at the state of your life when you arrived. It might not have all been shambles but I can guarantee you that there were areas in your existence that were devastated by your defects. What sane person wouldn't want these character traits gone? And, if you're not ready to give up one of your defects of character—say, maybe playing the victim—then you go right ahead and ride that donkey until it breaks. A defect, as noted above, is chaos against order, and it will fail, and it will hurt, and there will come a day when it will stop working for you and then you will come to your senses and you will let it go...but only after you've thoroughly had your ass kicked.

"Okay, but what am I to do? Nothing? Take no action whatsoever, stand there like a wounded animal waiting to be dispatched?"

"Of course not. I said you should not resist evil. I never said anything about not practicing good."

But before we discuss our upcoming actions, let's look at the prayer associated with the seventh step.

"My Creator, I am now willing that you should have all of me, good and bad. I pray that you now remove from me every single defect of character, which stands in the way of my usefulness to you and my fellows. Grant me strength, as I go out from here, to do your bidding."

Ah, a prayer to tidy things up before we move on. First, we acknowledge the source—a God to some, to others, the power inside—and the fact that we have accepted ourselves as we are. Dr. Carl Jung, the psychiatrist/psychotherapist, recognized that neurosis is the result of our attempt to avoid suffering; but here, we repress nothing, we don't fight the things that cause us pain, we accept them and we move forward. This prayer also reminds us that our main work is to be servants, useful to our fellow humans; again, if we go back to the supposed attributes of a loving God, we should serve the essences of life: truth, love, intelligence, soul, spirit and principle.

In one hand we have our defects and in the other our shortcomings; but wait, how are they different? I was told that a defect is what I had too much of, and a shortcoming is what I lack. Look at it this way: If I have too much pride then I'm short on humility. If my defect is gossip and shit talking, then I lack kindness. Basically, there is no difference between a defect and a shortcoming; they are just different ways to say the same thing. However, there *is* a difference in how they are remedied. If I'm asking for my defect to be removed, I'm asking for my overabundance of that defect to be taken away. If I ask for my shortcoming to be removed, I'm asking for my lack of an asset to be filled.

"Huh?'

"Yeah, I know it's a touch weird, but try this. If you and I are at the coffee shop and you say you're short a few bucks, I don't take the rest of your money. I reach into my pocket and toss you a couple. I fill your coffers so to speak. I removed your shortcoming by giving you more."

"Okay, I get that. But you don't really believe in this magic God thing so who helps you?"

"Who helps any of us really?"

I believe that when I become aware, or awake, that I'm able to channel a force from within, call it what you will; and when I'm asking for something to be removed, it's basically me exhibiting a willingness to practice better behavior, and I think that both believer and non-believer have the power to do that.

By not resisting evil, we give no power to our defects of character; instead, we put all of our will into nourishing their opposites. When we practice humility—being teachable, open-minded, and tolerant, it removes pride. Practicing forgiveness and understanding disintegrates wrath. Love dissolves resentment. Temperance vanishes gluttony. Action and willingness remove sloth. Sharing ourselves leaves no room for greed; and respect and complimentary behavior, come to be practiced instead of the lip-smacking creep of lust.

I was driving down the street one evening. I came upon a car with a flat tire. The occupants were two elderly women who weren't carrying phones—not that they could have successfully used them if they had had them.

"Don't you guys have phones?" I asked.

"Here in the car?" the driver said, "Of course not."

They did, however, have a spare tire and a jack in the trunk. I popped the trunk, grabbed the necessary items, and then I replaced their flat tire with one of those hard little donut jobs—you know, 50 miles or 50mph, whatever came first. Anyway, I got them fixed up and sent them on their way, but before they left, they offered me money—which I declined—and a car full of compliments, that I had a hard time swallowing. They were okay. I laughed after they left. Those two old ladies were calling me a blessing and a gift from God. Ha! If they only knew who just changed their tire. I was a liar. A cheat. A violent animal and a creep, but wait…not at that moment, I wasn't, to them I was perfect. I was without defect. I was a loving hand of God, sent to them when they needed me most. The thought startled me, and then I realized that what I needed to do was expand the perfection of that moment. Through service, I could be whole, healed, and without defect.

Alcohol has been called "spirits" because it mimics—although in a very weak and incomplete way—the feeling that we get when the spirit of love, or God, runs through us. Come on man, when the booze was working, you don't remember that cuddle-you-up feeling that came over you when the alcohol began to take over—that sense of ease and comfort? Of course you do, but it didn't last, and it nearly destroyed us. Since I mentioned Dr. Jung earlier, I'll give you

103

another example from him. Bill W. was big on corresponding and the well-known psychiatrist was one person with whom he was in contact with. In a letter to Bill, Dr. Jung wrote: "You see, alcohol in Latin is *spiritus* and you use the same word for the highest religious experience as well as for the most degrading poison. The helpful formula therefore is: *spiritus contra spiritum.*" We employ the Spirit against the spirits—or the booze, if you will.

We don't resist the drink: we don't fight or attempt to repress our alcoholism. Instead, we admit it, we know who we are, and we become channels of spirit...a force flowing through us that removes our desire to drink and heals us of a seemingly hopeless state of mind and body—as long as we stay in service and continue that flow.

The List...

There is a joke that floats around the program, a response from sponsor to sponsee.

"So...uh...I'm making a list of people I've harmed and uh...I'm not sure who to put on it."

"Okay," the sponsor says. "Where did you live?"

"I lived in Los Angeles."

"Great, start with the local phone book and then we'll grab the phone books of anywhere you might've traveled and we'll begin with the A's and work our way down."

The question isn't as much whom have we harmed, as it is, who didn't we? If we look at the whole of our lives—our unenlightened, selfish behavior—then we are basically going to amend our treatment of the world around us. We are to live as if we were reborn into the world of the spirit, accepting ourselves as new beings yet responsible for our old incarnation.

To amend something means: to put right; to change for the better; to alter formally by modification; to reform oneself.

With these definitions, we can see that it isn't just the gross wrongs that we are to settle, but basically, our whole attitude and outlook on life must change...

One of the reasons I like to combine Bill and Dr. Bob's inventories is that by doing so, I get a clearer picture of who I've harmed and how I need to amend those relationships.

When I first took an inventory, using the lines and columns that came directly out of the Big Book, I was a touch confused because it seemed as if my list was incomplete. Sure, I'd listed my resentments, my fears, and my sexual misconduct, but what about the times I was an asshole, or violent? What about those from whom I stole? What about my intolerance or my unwillingness to hear another's point of view? When I place Bill and Bob's inventories together, I get a complete list of my wrongs and a basic map of how I'm to right them. And, by the way, the dead count. Just because someone has left the physical world it doesn't mean that your debt to him or her is settled.

Returning That Which Was Stolen

There are those who make amends under sponsor direction "I was told to clean that up," but where is the heart in that? Do you not feel as if you've wronged them? Are you only doing this so you won't drink? That doesn't sound like a "spiritual awakening" to me; it sounds like following orders, not following your conscience. We discussed earlier the process of waking up and becoming aware, and what usually happens to one who remains asleep. If you don't think you've wronged someone then by all means don't go to him or her with some half-hearted apology or explanation. However, if you owe money connected to the wrong, return it—everyone enjoys getting repaid, but do so and keep your pie-hole shut.

I've mentioned the word sponsor a few times and I guess now is as good a time as any to discuss it. There is a wonderful twelve-step pamphlet on "sponsorship", if you're new, or even old, read it. It's a great guide. A sponsor is not your personal commander-in-chief. She or he does not own you. A sponsor's word is not law—their experience is their own and they should encourage you to find your own way. A sponsor is not paid for their services. A sponsor is not at your beck-and-call whenever you have a problem. A sponsor should be a closed-mouth friend and if they have no experience in what you're dealing with they should have no problem referring you to someone who has. That being said, if you blindly follow the dictates of another man or woman, you are what is known in the criminal industry as a "stooge;" however, in times of trouble, or indecision, if you don't seek wise counsel you are a fool.

This amends process is especially one where wise council is most needed. You don't want to do more harm by attempting to clean up old misdeeds unsuccessfully—or, attempt to clean up something that didn't need to be in the first place. I once had a guy try to make amends to me for what he thought.

"Hey man," he said, "I gotta talk to you."

"Yeah, what's up?"

"I wanted to tell you that I'm sorry for thinking you were a total asshole. For the last two years I've sat right here calling you a tool in my head."

"Wow," I said. "Who told you to do this?"

"My sponsor," he proudly replied.

"Well, you didn't owe me an amends before, but you do now. And, when your sponsor wakes up, you can send him over too."

We don't make personal amends for what we've been thinking— unless our thoughts have begat action. We make amends for thinking ill of another by thinking well of them—we imagine them as happy, whole, peaceful people. We wish the best for them, hoping above all that they receive enlightenment and love.

I think the best way for me to touch on the amends process is to give you a few examples of amends I've made. Each encounter is unique—different wrongs call for different rights. I had a friend who used to say that he never uses the word "sorry" when he makes an amend, and I understood his reasoning—most of us have said sorry too many times and it was never followed up by a change in behavior. However, some people want to hear that word, and if you are a true penitent then you are not there to dictate the terms of your amends to others.

An embarrassing amend

There was a woman who was, and still is, a friend of mine. I was at her home one day and while snooping around I found a box of old collectable books—they were her father's, from when he was a boy. I used to think that what was yours was mine, so I casually grabbed the box and loaded the books into my car. After I got sober, the books that had sat quietly on my shelf came to life. I'd walk by them and their colors brightened. I saw their true owner's face beneath the titles. They became so large that I could no longer look at them. They had to be returned. I called the woman I stole them from and asked if I could see her. I brought the books to her house. This woman had made it known to me that she admired me, even looked up to me, and now I came to her as a common thief. I was embarrassed.

"These are yours," I said. "I stole them from you." She was confused.

"Why?" she said. "I would've given them to you if you'd have asked."

I was embarrassed to face her, but I was wrong and I knew it. Those books were not the only objects that demanded—through their very presence to be returned to their rightful owners, and item by embarrassing item, those other objects also found their way home.

An amend without harm

Being a man isn't easy. Pride, ego, and looking good in front of other men are important facets of modern masculinity.

When I was drinking I enjoyed belittling others—not just physically harming them, but by attacking their manhood, embarrassing them in public situations. Some of these men buried the hurt, as I did—I was a master of filing things away in the locked, never to be looked at, recesses. I ran into one of these men in the market and I realized that I had taken from him, but I wasn't exactly sure how to proceed. I didn't have time to call a sponsor. I hadn't seen this man in years, and I haven't seen him since. Something needed to be said. I approached him and he acted happy to see me. He asked about my band and my writing. I let the conversation drift where he steered it, and then, when we were about to take our leave I said:

"You were always stronger than I was. I took the easy way out so many times. I didn't have the strength of character that you had. I didn't have it in me to be a good friend."

He looked at me for a moment and then I felt, almost saw, the power returned to him. He spoke to me in an almost fatherly manner.

"You did the best you could, Jack. I'm proud of what you've become."

He offered his hand—shook mine as a friend, and then he walked away.

Sometimes we need to admit our wrongs in a way that doesn't re-open old wounds. It's not up to me to make someone face something that they've discarded. Tact, and prudence are necessary in these cases.

110

An amend without fear

I'm never surprised when I'm confronted with a wrong that I supposedly committed—I've operated in blackouts more times than once. I've also forgotten more wrongs than I could ever set right.

A woman's boyfriend came to me. It was a casual talk at first, but then he said, "You've got unfinished business with my girl. You need to straighten that out."

I knew immediately what he meant. It was an episode that had taken place at my house—one that I'd thought nothing of. My moral fiber, in my drinking life, was best summed up as dangerously sociopathic. I loved this woman. I had no idea that I had hurt her that badly. I went to her. She explained to me that she had been in therapy for what I'd done. I asked her how I could make it right. I told her that if she wanted to press charges, I wouldn't fight it. I'd plead guilty. I wouldn't drag it out.

"That's not necessary Jack," she said. "I just needed to know that you were sorry for what you'd done. I needed you to be responsible for the pain that you caused me."

I couldn't have felt more responsible, or more willing to take whatever step she needed for her comfort—regardless of what it did to me.

There is a great Chuck C. quote that I'll mention here, "I have to be willing to go to any lengths if need be, but the program hasn't asked that of me."

An amend to an institution

I was a real shit when it came to schools, and other than the personal amends that I would have to make to the teachers and various administrators of these institutions, I owed a general amend to the institution of education itself. The way I've handled this is by volunteering my time in classrooms. I have been the guest speaker in political assemblies, drug awareness rallies, and even the guest literary lecturer on occasion. I pay back, or modify my old behavior, by offering myself in service. I think one of the best parts of this sort of amends is: I don't need to tell anyone why I do it. I sometimes hear others give their, "Hey, I'm here because I was such a bad-ass in school." spiel, but I don't. I roll in like just another square off the street—show up, do what's asked, and then leave.

An amend unaccepted

At times, I've tried to make amends and they aren't accepted. Sometimes the pain that we have caused sits too deep—you may be willing, but your victim is also ill, and they might refuse to relinquish the hurt. In these cases, I do my best to right the wrong. If they don't want to see me, I don't press the matter. If they don't want to talk to me, I sometimes send a letter or an email. I've sent checks that were cashed but never acknowledged, and I've been told that they're glad I'm sober but please, go be sober elsewhere. Once again, this is a matter of willingness to right the wrong, an understanding that the amends are on their terms, and an acknowledgement that the universe does not stop and start at my command.

An amend to the dead

I mentioned before that the dead do count, and I've found that they will not let you rest until you face what you have done to them. I had a terrible relationship with my father. We fought constantly. He was overweight, a smoker, a stress case, and a functioning alcoholic—meaning, he had a family and went to work. I wanted nothing to do with his authority and I was full of anger toward him. My father died in 1984. I was upset at first but then a day or two after he passed I put his clothes in garbage bags and readied them for the trash. On the day of my father's funeral I went surfing. I refused to attend the burial. Sometime after his death there was a court case. It was an insurance claim issue—my father had had his heart attack at work, and my mother, who had no means of support other than my father's military pension sought damages. Depositions were taken. My mother said that the stress from my father's job hastened his death. The employer countered with, "It was stress alright, but not from us, it was from him, his punk-rock crazy son." They blamed me for my father's demise. I used their accusation as a tool to stay loaded—more self-pity to fan the fires of alcoholism. When I got sober the ghost of my father came to call. Every time I heard the word dad I became uncomfortable, uneasy. I mentioned this to a few well-intentioned members of the program and I was told that his death was not my fault, that he had done it to himself.

That brought me no peace. Something in that explanation didn't seem right. I went to his grave. My father was all those things that I mentioned above: a stress case, an overweight alcoholic, a smoker, etc., but I also was what I was—an out-of-control son, an angry punk, a thief, and a vicious cowardly animal. I knelt at my father's grave and I asked him for forgiveness. I told him that I was sober and that I now had a daughter. I expressed my regret for the way I treated him and I thanked him for what he gave to me. After a few moments of quiet reflection I rose from his grave, and I realized that that was the longest conversation I had ever had with him. I'm now able to see my father for what he was, a man who did the best he could with what he had, and the anger that I held has been replaced with a healthy emptiness at my loss.

An amend which the universe dictates

I've told you that I don't believe in the "Magic God" but I will admit that there are forces, or currents, that travel in this world, connections that are not easily explained...as in, when the universe decides its time for you to become compliant.

When I was a teen I had a girlfriend. She was pretty, innocent as could be, and totally unprepared for me. I was the boyfriend from hell. Her parents, good Christian people, took more of my shit than I would have ever stood for—even sober, I've slapped around a couple of my underage daughter's late-night suitors. Her parents were probably overjoyed when I disappeared from her life.

114

Years passed. I got sober. I figured the best way to make amends to those folks was to leave them alone—at times a very acceptable plan, however...

I have a friend who was a golfer. He was about thirty-six years sober and he was to meet three friends for a round of 18 holes. His friends had car trouble and never showed. He decided he'd play anyway and he jumped on with three players unknown to him. During the course of the game, he noticed that one of the guys was upset and not playing well. My friend, being a good member of the program, offered his assistance in the way of a kind word and then a sympathetic ear. It turned out that the troubled man had a son who was taking drugs, going to jail, and enjoying a bit of the old punk rock. My friend broke his anonymity.

"I've been sober a long time," he said, "and I might have a friend who could help your boy. We should call Jack."

"Jack Grisham?" said the man.

"Yeah, do you know him?"

"Jack introduced me to my wife."

The golfer was married to the sister of the pretty young girl I used to date. My friend gave me this man's number and I made the call. After a few, "How've you beens?" and such, the conversation switched to the son and I offered to talk with him.

"He's at his grandparents," the man said. "Do you need the number?"

"No," I replied. "I know it."

The boy was living with the parents of my ex. I had called that number often. It was etched in my heart. I rang him that afternoon. The grandma answered. I stammered.

"Uh...Mrs. Jones?" I said.

"Jack?" She replied. "I never thought that you'd be doing me a favor."

Some people never do anything without first running it by a sponsor, it's totally fear-based, but when new, I understand their not wanting to fuck things up. But I say if the universe arranges your meeting—if the man or woman that you haven't seen since childhood, the one you owe an amends to, is standing right next to you in a line—then by all means you must go, dive in, and do your best to repair the relationship. I know you might be afraid of screwing things up, but if your heart is in the right place—or even nudging its way there—go without fear. You might make a mess, it might get worse, even turn into a fistfight, but if you've properly worked a first step and you trust in whatever you believe in, you won't get drunk over it and you'll probably be pleasantly surprised at the outcome.

An amend I can't make

Sometimes there are amends we can't make—willingness aside, for whatever reason, we never obtain closure.

When I was new, and sadly not so new, I struggled with fidelity. When I fucked up, as I so often did, I would go to my significant other and come clean. I felt better; a weight was taken off my chest. She felt worse—a hurt and betrayal had been dumped upon her shoulders. A member of the program pulled me aside one day. She told me that we have no right to hurt another to make ourselves feel better. We must be hard on ourselves and easy on others.

116

"And then, maybe," she said, "your lack of relief might just stop you from doing it again."

"My lack of relief?"

One day, in my unenlightened life, I beat a man senseless. A friend and I chased him after he had spit at our car—which he had done only after we'd swerved at him. We caught up to him on a lawn by the high school. His hands were full of books and papers. It looked as if he was going to night school to better his life. When we were through with him he barely moved. His books and papers were torn and thrown about, his mouth bleeding; his body was crumpled on the grass. I was lucky that we didn't kill him. I don't know who he was. I have no way to reach him. I have prayed, asked the universe for intercession, and I've received no comfort. I can't get his face to leave my head—the look in his eyes as he cried. I can't say that I've never used violence since, I've instinctively struck out many times, well into sobriety, but I will say that consciously I'm sickened by it. I do my best to practice peace.

There are those who hesitate on this action—they fight the process of making amends. If you truly regret your wrongs, you will have no trouble facing them. If you're not sure if you're wrong, see if the image of the person leaves your mind; if it doesn't, if their face hovers like the noon sun in your memory, you'll know what to do.

When We Realized We Were Wrong

No sober member works a perfect program—oh, wait, I mean…we all do, because chances are most of us are screwing this thing up one way or another—a touch of pride creeps in, a sliver of lust, a rash of fear and, at times, we act on it, it's expected. If they didn't think we were going to wander off course a touch, the step would read "…and *if* we were wrong" not "*when* we were wrong."

The founders of the twelve-step program built failure, or at least the impossibility of thorough completion, into the steps. If you look at Step Ten, Eleven, and Twelve, you will see: "When we were wrong", "Sought to improve". and "Tried to carry the message." So basically, they're saying, "We're going to screw up, our contact isn't good enough, and sometimes, we might not get the message through." It's beautiful. It encourages humility and a beginner's mind. It teaches us that these steps have room for limitless expansion and that we never complete this process.

At times newer members have asked me the question, "What step are you on?" It's a question that they probably heard in their recovery house, or around the meetings. It doesn't bother me if they're implying, "What step are you focusing on?" because, I'm constantly studying this process and attempting a greater understanding. But, at times it seems as if newer members assume that you must repeat some of these steps, and that you can also only do one of them at a time. Lets look at that more closely.

As a recovered member of the program, can I say I'm on Step One? No, of course I can't. How could I say I'm powerless over alcohol? The book tells me I'm not—I've connected to an inner resource and power has been returned. Is my life unmanageable? Nope. I live by the dictates of my enlightenment. You know my God: love, kindness, spirit and soul. I'm disciplined when I fall out of accordance with those traits. Do I fuck up sometime? Yeah, see Step Ten.

Can I say I'm on Step Two? No. I'm here, I'm doing the work and, if I didn't believe in this process, and I hadn't been restored to sanity, I'd be somewhere else—quite possibly chasing a drink.

What about three, can I say I'm on Step Three? No. I've moved ahead. The minute you start that inventory and head down this road you've moved past that decision. I'm living this life. I can't go back and make a decision to do what I'm already doing.

Can I say I'm on Step Four? No, I can't, because I've already completed it, and any further inventory I take falls under Step Ten. There are members who do an annual housecleaning, but I'd be careful with this. The sickest people in the program are the ones who are constantly studying themselves. You can't get out of self by studying self.

Okay, how about Step Five then? Can I say I'm on that one? Nope. I've done it, and if you've done it you can't say it either, unless the person asking the question just busted into your confessional. Do I share my life, good or bad, with my sponsor or mentor? Of course, I stay current and connected. But when doing so it falls under Step Ten.

Step Six or Seven, I hear people say they're active on those, can I say I'm working them? I told you earlier, we acknowledge and move on. Once again, Step Ten is where we live.

Can I say I'm on Step Eight? No. If you did Step Four properly you already have your list. And if another name comes up, or you left something out, see Step Ten.

Maybe Nine, Can I say I'm on that step? Yes, as we discussed earlier we amend our behavior and we are never through with that metamorphosis—unless we've decided we're done—in which case we're no longer growing. If you don't grow, you go. We have our personal amends, but we also have a living amends, and you'd be surprised how forgotten hurts often come to light.

Can I say I'm on Step Ten? Yes, and we should all be. The moment you wake up—accept your alcoholism—you should be on the look out for selfish, self-centered behavior—making it a constant vigil. It is asinine for your guide, sponsor, or whatever you choose to call them, not to get you on this step as soon as possible. Get used to checking yourself, it will become a way of life.

Can I say I'm on Step Eleven? I hope so. The purpose of those steps is to connect you to a Higher Power, so you better start trying to cuddle up with it. I found that when I awoke I was filled with a hunger and a yearning for knowledge and connection. It's been said that we are created, if you will, to seek. If you're awake, you'll feel it, a desire for something more...

Can I say I'm on Step Twelve? Yes, if you've moved towards a lifestyle based on giving instead of getting, truly altruistic—then being of service becomes the fiber of your soul. Those who are awake act like it. They beam. They share. They look after their fellows. Do they always do this? Of course not, but more often than not they exude this spirit. Before I was awake the chances of you rolling up on me while I was up to no good was probably ninety-nine times out of a hundred. There would be the few odd incidences

121

where I was being helpful, or kind, but they were greatly outnumbered by the harmful, self-centered enterprises that I was usually engaged in.

When we begin this process—right after we've made our third step decision to live in this manner—we immediately commence with Steps Ten, Eleven, and Twelve as we concurrently work the others. As the Big Book says on pg. 84, "We vigorously commenced this way of living as we cleaned up the past."

"Whoa, hold up Jack. My sponsor says that I can't give away what I don't have."

"Yeah, he probably says a bad relationship will get you drunk too."

"Well…as a matter of fact, he does."

"God help us."

A bad relationship never got anyone drunk. The program is filled with people in bad relationships—as is life. You will also hear people blame their drunkenness on all sorts of things, as if the drink crawled up their legs and poured itself down their throats. There are plenty of excuses to drink; however, I've found that people in recovery usually drink because they've never properly worked a first step, never conceded, and then taken the action necessary to connect them with a higher power. As for you having nothing to give, what about a smile? What about getting someone a cup of coffee or offering him or her a chair? What about saying hello to a new person, welcoming an out-of-town visitor, or helping to clean up after the meeting? You have more than enough to give. To be honest, I'd much rather see a newcomer doing service work at the coffee bar than studying lines in the Big Book.

When taking Step Ten we're supposed to watch for selfishness, dishonesty, resentment and fear. When these defects pop up we go to a meeting and waste an hour of other people's time by bitching and whining about how fucked-up we are...

No.

We don't.

When those defects arise we go to "God", or whatever power we choose— and make the acknowledgement to our higher self that this is not the way we want to live. Then, we discuss them with another member, clean it up, and go back to being of service— continuing with our lives. We don't fight it. We don't dwell on it. We don't spend hours in a meeting discussing how sick we are.

We see it.

We acknowledge it.

We clean it up.

We move on.

Once again, no power is given to the defect. Step Ten includes one of my favorite lines, it reads, "and we have ceased fighting anything or anyone—even alcohol."

Let that sit for a moment.

Anything. Anyone. Even alcohol.

You don't have the strength to overpower the "evil". You can't hide from the booze. You can't work on your character defects. Any attempt you make to fight is futile.

"But I feel sad."

"Great, be sad. What makes you think you should always feel happy?"

"But I'm an alcoholic."

"Finally. Now, stop trying to fix it. Connect and move on. Practice being sober."

Step Ten is about emotional sobriety. It is about a life of maturity, being grown-up, it is not a life characterized by the fears and clenched fists, of a spoiled child.

Bill writes:

"We are not fighting it, neither are we avoiding temptation. We feel as though we had been placed in a position of neutrality—safe and protected. We have not even sworn off. Instead, the problem has been removed. It does not exist for us. We are neither cocky nor are we afraid."

This is an example of acceptance—to just be what we are. To see others as they are. To see the world as it is.

The English language can be confusing. Some words have two or even three literal meanings. Acceptance can be defined as: accepting a gift, approving of a person, place or thing, or as belief. However, it is this last definition that is most important to the alcoholic—a person in full flight from reality—for we'll do all we can to fight or change a thing that can't be beaten or will not change. Our first experience with this was when we struggled with our illness—we tried everything we could to prove ourselves non-alcoholic. We then struggled as we learned that our selfish will didn't work—we tried to control the world and its inhabitants. Then we tried this with ourselves—we fought what we were, or are—as we tried to make ourselves better, almost beyond human. We couldn't receive help for our alcoholism until we accepted that there was nothing we could do to change it—we hit a hopeless state. We couldn't, or wouldn't, seek spiritual aid until we tried everything we could to control the world—we ran our lives into the ground. We couldn't move forward in our emotional growth until we accepted the fact that we are human. At times we behave so valiantly and at other times we are so much less than expected. We are neither good nor bad but a rainbow of actions between.

Acceptance, or to "resist not evil", does not mean we give up, it doesn't mean we approve of what's happening, and it doesn't mean we take the situation as a gift—although, you can use any situation to learn, but that's next level shit.

"Can you give us an example?"

Okay, I was giving a talk in a state institution. I was approached by a man whom I thought had been released a year earlier—I called him on it.

"Hey, bud," I said. "I thought you were out of here?"

"I was, Jack, but I gave a dirty test, so they gave me another six months, but I can do six months. It's cool."

"Acceptance, yeah?"

"You bet. Just working the program."

"At the risk of getting shanked," I said. "May I give you my opinion?"

"Yeah."

"As long as you think you can do six months you're going to keep doing six months. It's not until the thought of doing another six months becomes so unacceptable that you'll do something different."

In this case, our delinquent friend was using acceptance as approval, when he should've been using acceptance as belief and then applying disapproval to activate positive actions. I was a restraining-order alcoholic. I refused to believe that they didn't want me around. "They're just mad," I thought. I'll wait a day and go back. Acceptance means belief—I'm not welcome there.

"But, I'm powerless over my drunken husband. I'm powerless over people, places, and things."

No, not if you have a program, and a Higher Power, then you can't be powerless...control-less, yes, but powerless, no. People mistake an inability to control with a lack of power, but they're not the same. I can't make my defiant significant other straighten up and do as I say, but I can check myself, seek help, move if need be, alter my perception of the problem, or stop buying into the craziness; I have a world of possible solutions at my fingertips. That's not being powerless.

The heading of this chapter reads, "And when we realized we were wrong." It's a joke—I'm screwing with the wording of the Tenth Step. The alcoholic isn't always quick to see and admit where they've stepped out of line. Sometimes, it takes some of us a few hours, days, or even weeks to admit and repair our wrongs.

I was twelve years sober. I had my children in the car. My oldest, Anastasia, was fourteen. The baby, Georgia, was about two. It was seven in the morning. I had been out looking at the surf. I was late. The girls needed to go to school and daycare. We were heading down the Pacific Coast Highway. I was speeding—not crazy fast, but definitely a speed that would get you popped. I was agitated. My ex-wife can be a bit of a...uh...forceful, and I knew I was going to get shit for taking the kids when they should've been home. About a mile from my house I got red-lighted—a motorcycle cop had been hiding near the service road.

"Dad?"—came the voice of my fourteen-year-old, skin-headed, junior punk daughter. "The cops are behind you."

I looked in the rear-view mirror without slowing. "Yeah," I said. "Fuck him."

At that moment, my daughter, who later bloomed into a wonderful chip off her father's craziness, realized that her anarchy patch was made of cloth and her dad was made of the real thing.

"I gotta get you guys home," I said. "He can wait."

I waved the cop off and kept driving. He hit me with the squawking horn—the one used for motorists who are too deaf to hear. I ignored it.

"Dad?"

"Look," I said. "When I pull up to the house you grab your sister and jump out. Get inside and get ready for school." The siren was now blasting behind the vehicle.

I pulled up in front of my house—a mile from where he first lit me up. He hopped off his bike and fast approached my window.

"What the fuck are you..."

127

"Ana," I said, ignoring him. "Get your sister and go." I looked at the cop. "Hey, champ," I said. "I think I got a tail-light out. Why don't you go take a peep? Ana, move!"

My daughter bailed out of the car with her sister and I exited to argue with the wanna-be voice of authority who thought he had the fucking right to stop me. I'm a free man, goddamn it. I was lucky he didn't call for back-up—if I were the officer in charge I would've beaten my ass and tossed me in for resisting—a charge I've garnered before. After a bit of back and forth between the officer and myself, he wrote me for everything he could—except evading, and then he handed me the ticket and sped off. I entered the house furious and then…I realized I was wrong. Now, most normal folks realize they're wrong when they see the speed limit sign and notice they're a few clicks over. I don't. As I've said before, "I've been fucking up my life for so long that the kids think I'm keeping it real." I was going to have to clean this mess up.

The officer's name was on the ticket. I knew that I could go to the station and set up a time to meet with him. Two weeks later and I was still thinking about it. Sometimes promptly isn't so prompt with this alcoholic.

I was walking with my ex-wife along the beach path. I still had the officer in my head. I knew I was going to have to face him at some point, but I was not yet tortured enough by my conscience to go find him.

"Oh, shit," I said.

"What?"

"The cop. The one I fucked with is right there."

He was parked. Sitting on his motorcycle. Hiding behind a sign. Waiting to spring, as he had done that morning. The universe deemed it necessary for me to come clean. I looked at my ex-wife.

"I'm going in."

She stopped walking and I approached the officer. He made me as I moved forward and he hopped off his bike. He dropped his right hand to his hip, hovering over his service revolver—he straight-armed his left.

"Okay," he said. "That's far enough."

He thought I was coming in for round two—rolling in hot. I stopped.

"It's not like that, man," I said. "I just wanted to tell you that I was sorry. You're out here all day busting your balls and I had no right to be an asshole to you. I was the one who was speeding. I was wrong." I finished talking and I started to turn away.

"Hey," he said. "Hang on a minute."

He relaxed his stance and moved toward me. He held out his hand. I could see that his eyes were a touch misty when I reached out to shake with him.

"Twenty years on the force, " he said, "and that's the first time anyone has ever apologized to me."

Conscious Contact

The Eleventh Step says that we need to improve our conscious contact with God—conscious contact—as in a direct communication with the almighty? In the twenty-six years that I've been clean, I have never heard a message from a deity. No heavenly voice has echoed through my home. No burning bush, or winged man appeared before me. I have yelled to the stars and stood penitent and naked in the desert—alone, always alone. The Eleventh Step asks me to look within—examine my conscience more so than my contact.

This step, before all others, molded me into the agnostic I am today. It has not brought me closer to an entity called God; if anything, it has made me doubt His existence. Even the wording in the book suits an agnostic more so than it does a believer. Yes, there is mention of God, "ask Him for this", "He gave us brains", but then what? We're directed back to self, we are to trust our instincts and our inner voice. There is no promise that "He" will materialize before us—everything depends on our relationships with those around us.

There is an interesting twist that is about to take place. We couldn't take a ninth step until we had finished our fourth, and that's a fairly elementary conclusion, but, can we really take a Tenth Step, if we're not actively engaged with Step Eleven?

On pg. 86 of the Big Book there is a paragraph that is often mistaken as a Tenth-Step checklist. It says that we review our day:

have we been resentful, selfish, dishonest, or afraid? Do we owe an apology? We're asked to look within, to practice constant awareness of where our behavior stands in regard to those around us. We might have had a flash of awareness in the beginning of this recovery process, an, "oh-my-god-I'm-really-screwed" moment, but we need to stay awake; lest we drift back to sleep…and for us, to sleep is not to dream, it is to walk toward death.

If you're not awake, it's impossible to see where you've been wrong. If you're wrapped up inside a world that revolves around you in the haze of a self-centered mist, how can you claim to be recovered? In the Eleventh Step we practice awareness—reviewing the day to see where we might have missed the mark—and then, when we recognize a wrong, we use our intuition to seek a solution, be it an apology or some other form of amends. Then, we turn back to the Tenth Step and clean it up. The two steps, Ten and Eleven, worked congruently—awareness, a thought for right action, and an implementation of that thought.

I've heard old-timers tell the newcomer not to think. "Let me do your thinking for you," they say. "Your brain got you into this mess…it can't get you out." I wonder how many people those old-timers have inadvertently killed? I sure hope that if you're one of those people telling "your" newcomer not to think, that you have your ass strapped to that newcomer round the clock, for there will come a time that they will be alone and due to your prideful "I am your God" sponsorship, you will have left them without the tools needed to overcome the obstacle. There is a quote by Albert Einstein and it is:

"We can't solve problems by using the same kind of thinking we used when we created them."

And we're not, we've awakened, we've become aware that a life based on selfish will is one of pain and strife. Our thinking *has* changed—maybe only slightly as we are still new, but it's changed enough to move forward. We've had an awakening and been given a new mind and now, a new way of thinking. On pg. 86, Bill hits us with this:

"On awakening **let us think** about the twenty-four hours ahead. We **consider our plans** for the day. Before we begin, we ask God to **direct our thinking**, especially asking that it be divorced from self-pity, dishonest or self-seeking motives. Under these conditions we can **employ our mental faculties** with assurance, for after all God gave us **brains to use**. Our **thought-life** will be placed on a much higher plane when our **thinking** is cleared of wrong motives."

Seven times he asks us to think. Seven times, in one paragraph—read it. If I turned a paragraph like that into an editor I'd be called up on redundancy. Bill seemingly didn't care. He wanted us to develop our thinking, especially, "that it be divorced from self-pity, dishonest or self-seeking motives." Learning to think takes practice—not deferral. Since you like examples, I'll give you this:

"I'm fat as shit right now, should I go to the gym and hire a trainer to work out for me? Hell no, because at the end of a year he'd be in great shape, and I'd still be fighting to tie my shoes."

I have a long list of friends who have died, a majority of them from this illness. I miss them—terribly. There are people in the

133

program who treat those who get loaded as if they were somehow subhuman, less than, and their wisdom and words are in someway invalid. I can learn as much from the new man, or the continual "relapser", as I can from the long-timer. Each of us has a distinct path, who knows where they all lead? Some of our roads lead back to the bottle.

I was speaking with my present mentor, a man sober some forty-six years, and we were talking about a friend. An acquaintance of ours had just died during a relapse. When sober, this member had helped more people than I'll possibly ever touch.

"They say to stick with the winners," my mentor said. "But getting loaded didn't make him a loser."

I wish others could have this sort of sponsorship. Don't be so quick to condemn and judge.

I gained part of my understanding of the Eleventh Step from a man who could not stop drinking. Yes, he had periods of sobriety, but he was never able to connect with that of which he so knowledgeably spoke.

"Jack," he said to me, "have you ever heard of the term *sotto voce*? It's a musical term."

"Ha!" I said. "Are you fucking kidding me? Do you know what kind of band I'm in? It's punk rock baby—'fuck the government', and 'give me free cheese.'"

He laughed.

"It means the voice beneath," he said. "When you listen closely, under the static, there's a quiet voice which tells you the truth. Most alkies never take the time to listen. That's why so many of us die."

Yeah, maybe that's why he died.

134

Meditation, to a Christian-based person, is more of a contemplative practice. I've been to Dr. Bob's house. The good proctologist from the Midwest had no orange robes or gongs in his living room. He did however have a Bible. The meditation that was done there was a reading and then a reflection of how that passage could fit into their lives—how we can take that knowledge and put it to use in our servitude. If, as Bill wrote on pg. 23, "...the main problem of the alcoholic centers in his mind rather than his body" then it's of utmost importance that this area be treated. The Eleventh Step is the way we arrest our old negative thinking. We replace those fear-based thoughts with new ideas—passages focusing on love and service, faith and connection—and our old notions are carried away as the words of spirit fill our hearts and minds. As a word of note, your reading doesn't necessarily have to come from a so-called spiritual teacher; it can come from anywhere or anyone. In the case of the Eleventh Step, it's the message not the messenger. Let me try a stanza for you; how about something from Thomas Merton—

"Our idea of God tells us more about ourselves than about Him."

After reading Merton's words, I'd sit quietly for a moment and then look within; the thought might progress something like this:

"What is my idea of God? I don't believe in a deity, but I do believe in love and connection. Does my unwillingness to believe in God stem from the way I was raised, my connection to my parents? Or, does believing in ideals, rather than an incarnation, mean that I may have begun to grow away from my self-seeking nature and become willing to believe in a power that is without definition…"

Spending a few moments of my day in pursuit of enlightened thought is healthy and productive, it's calming, and it brings wisdom—a tool that can be well used in service. Let's try a reading of a more practical nature.

"Miss no single opportunity of making some small sacrifice, here by a smiling look, there by a kindly word; always doing the smallest right and doing it all for love." Therese de Lisieux

As before, a quiet moment, but in the case of this stanza I would think more on the general ideal than I would each word as I did before—again, the progression of thought:

"My service doesn't have to be a grand gesture or a loud statement of faith—if I keep love in my heart, and express that in the simplest of my daily moves, it's enough. I should remember that the demonstration of my faith is something that is to be practiced in full at all levels…love, remember love."

After I read this piece and explored my thoughts, I would offer maybe a short prayer or intention, that I remember this stanza throughout the day. The more I practice this way of thinking, the easier it becomes.

If you attend a regular meeting, as I do, you'll find that each meeting's theme is usually based on a reading—a passage from a book of daily meditations. The piece is read aloud and then we're supposed to discuss it—focusing on the message and how it applies to our lives. If the meeting doesn't include a specific reading, a topic

136

is usually put forth and we're to speak on it. The purpose of these exercises is to begin training the mind—sharpening focus and intention. I know you think you're having trouble at work. I know you're stressed out over the behavior of your kids. I know you feel fearful and depressed, but just for a few moments, put all that aside and concentrate on the reading—actively discuss the topic. It will change your life.

I had an old timer ask me one day, "Who's running the show, buddy, you or your mind?" For years my unconscious mind ran the show, with no thought of others or how my actions would affect them. I was the alpha to the omega. You existed to please me. On autopilot I tore through the day waging a self-centered war with the world. When I woke up, being torn from my slumber and rocketed into a dimension that was now uncomfortably populated by others, it took work to corral the demon that was my head—I needed to practice conscious contact with an enlightened self. I needed to practice focus, connection and service.

I had a friend who believed the newcomer should be encouraged to share whatever they wanted in a meeting. "I'm just glad they're participating," he'd say. His opinion was one of hot debate between us. I would've thrown hot coffee on him if I still behaved like that—sorry, I was teasing. He said he liked to hear the newcomers' rambling incoherent chatter about their problems—it made him feel better. First off, I don't need to hear your pain to make me feel better; I live a great life and that does it for me. Secondly, it's my belief that the quicker a new person can learn to focus and get ahold of their head the better. If you encourage a newcomer to run with their un-mastered thoughts, you're basically endorsing a tool that will ultimately kill them.

137

There's a great line in *Bull Durham*—the Kevin Costner, Tim Robbins film. In the movie Costner's character is an aging baseball catcher who's philosophically sound, but who never made it to the big leagues, other than a short stint in "the show". Tim Robbins plays a young pitching phenomenon. It's Costner's job to season the young man—sponsor him if you will. The scene I'll refer to is one in which they first meet. The two men have had a disagreement and they've stepped out to an alley to settle their differences. Instead of beating on the young man, Costner's character hands him a baseball and in front of a crowd of onlookers he tells Robbins to hit him with it.

"C'mon, Meat," he says, "you can't hit me 'cause you're starting to think about it already, you're starting to think how embarrassing it'll be to miss, how all these people would laugh. C'mon, Rook—show me that million-dollar arm 'cause I'm getting a good idea about that five cent head."

Robbins threw the ball. He missed.

We can have all the talent in the world, but if our heads are loose, we might as well piss that promise down the drain. An alcoholic head will tell you that you don't have a problem. It will tell you that those who say they love you are liars. It will tell you that the grass is greener and the new object of your affection will somehow be kinder, gentler, sweeter, and more understanding than your wife. It will tell you that your husband and your kids would be better off without you. It will tell you that you would be better off dead.

I have a friend who lived up north. One day while walking down the street he got a message from "God"—a voice came to him.

"Sell everything and go to Vegas," it said.

138

He called me that afternoon. I suggested he seek help—a psychiatrist (or a good "lobotomist"). He did. He went to months of therapy and yet the voice wouldn't stop. Incessantly it dictated what his actions should be. One morning, I received a call.

"Hey, bro," he said. "I'm doing it. I fucking liquidated man. I'm going."

"Are you talking about that voice?" I said.

"Yeah man. I sought help. I did what you said. It wouldn't quit. So I'd be a fool not to go."

How could I argue? I told him to stay in touch—let me know how it went down. Liquidated, he was worth a touch over sixty grand. He got on a plane. At the Vegas airport, the voice told him to go to Caesars. He went. At the hotel, the voice told him to go to the roulette wheel and lay everything on 19 red. *Everything*. He did. The croupier rolled the wheel. The small metal ball was dropped on the track. It spun round and round purposely looking for a numbered home—divinely inspired. The wheel slowed. The ball bounced twice and then came to rest, in…31 black.

The voice of "God" said, "Shit."

I would suggest learning how to be the master of your mind as soon as possible.

"But my sponsor said that I'm not there yet. I'm not on the Eleventh Step. I need someone's help who has time and has worked this program."

You don't need a sponsor's help to work this program. You don't need someone who has gone before you to sit with you and explain these steps—It's nice, but not necessary. You don't need to attend a meeting every day. That being said, we're lucky we have people who have been sober for many years. We should be grateful for their experience. We're lucky we have numerous meetings to go to—if you do—but you don't need it. We have the Big Book. The directions within are simple and easy to follow. Sadly, when I say this, I'm branded as a subversive or a heretic, but I'm only repeating what the book says. Bill writes "...though you be but one man with this book in your hand." In the Big Book Bill brags about groups of "twos and threes and fives of us...". They didn't have members with long-term sobriety in the beginning. They didn't have round-the-clock meetings and Internet access. They didn't have cell phones or even answering machines. Do you think there was something they had that you don't? Do you think these steps work only if you're in a metropolitan area, or if your sponsor has a year or more? You either believe in this process or you don't. No member needs any special circumstances or requirements to recover. If you are alone, Bill tells you how to grow a fellowship around you. Where is your dependence? Is it on your sponsor, the meetings, the group, or your Higher Power? You tell me. Better yet, tell yourself.

In the Eleventh Step we begin with a hunch, and it gradually turns into a working part of the mind. Bill says that we'll make mistakes, but that's okay, we have a process to clean them up if we do. As I said before, a bad decision or a hunch that goes astray does not mean you're going to get drunk—we've been restored to sanity, we don't think a drink will bring relief or comfort. We know it's not our solution. Live your life untethered and free, for after all; don't you think you were in the cage of alcoholism long enough?

To return to the small voice, the *sotto voce*, I will place myself in the car—not the time I was red-lighted and sped away, but a time a bit further on. A time where my meditation bore fruit.

I was driving down the street, hustling to get nowhere in particular, when a man pulled out in front of me without looking. I had to step heavy on my brakes. I almost slammed into the back of his car. The orchestra came alive. The great kettledrums began.

"Kill him! Kill him! Kill him!" they pounded. And then the brass broke loose—the trumpets and trombones blaring.

"Pull alongside and flip him off, pull alongside and flip him off." And then the strings joined the din—the cellos and the violins weaving in sweet concoctions of revenge.

"Get in front and slow down, get in front and slow down."

The orchestra was demanding reprisal, screaming for the head of that errant driver and then...quiet and low...a voice slow and steady whispered from beneath and then grew.

"It's okay, Jack," the voice said. "Let it go. You're in no hurry, and there's nowhere that important to go."

I smiled and waved as I passed.

I've told you before that I don't believe in a "Magic God." I don't believe in miracles, or in a deity who finds you that perfect parking place but at the same time lets children get slaughtered and innocents suffer; but I do believe there are many forces working that we're unaware of, and I'm open to anything. I believe that the more we become interested in our fellow humans—starting by checking ourselves and later, developing our conscious contact and getting more in tune with the world and those around us—we begin to develop a new sense—a clairvoyance, if you will. Now, don't think

141

I'm going off the deep end. If I haven't lost you yet, I surely don't want to lose you now. But have you ever been with a friend, or a loved one, and you just knew that something wasn't right? They hadn't telescoped any negativity through word or deed and yet something didn't sit well with you; so you reached out and they admitted that something had indeed been troubling them.

It was a weekday. It had been raining intermittently but now the rain was more of a heavy mist that hung over the ocean. I was waiting for Becky, the letter carrier. I liked to speak with her when she came by. I walked out onto the porch. On the sidewalk, in front of my house stood two people, a woman in her mid-fifties, and a young man who looked to be at the hard end of his thirties. They each carried a backpack, and the woman, a small suitcase.

"Do you know where the hostel is?" she asked. The building she was referring to had been vacated last year.

"It's gone," I said.

The young man seemed oblivious but the woman was obviously frustrated and tired. The rain crept back over the coast road.

"We took the bus here," she said. "There's not another for an hour."

I stared at them a moment, felt the first drops hit my skin, and then I asked if they would like to come inside and wait. I offered them tea—they were foreigners, you know how those people love tea. They sat at my small kitchen table as I filled the kettle and lit the stove. She was inquisitive; he was in a quiet, withdrawn space. I noticed a gold cross hanging from her neck.

"I'm one of those," I said.

I don't usually claim this. Not that I'm embarrassed, I'm stronger than being ashamed of my beliefs, but normally, when you say you're a follower of Christ to a Christian, you usually get asked if you've been saved. It's like they don't have anything else to share. So many great teachings and you threaten me with fire? My guest didn't offend. She touched her necklace as she would the hand of a loved one and she asked me "Why?" I didn't go into the whole story. When you meet someone new, and they're sitting in your home for the first time, it's best that you not regale them with stories of assault, bomb making, alcoholism, sexual misconduct, and drug use—things can get a bit uncomfortable if you do. I told her that at the time I was struggling and I needed something to lift me—bring me up so to speak. I told her a clean version of the garage incident, the one where I caught my daughter smoking.

"Is there a hotel near here?" she asked.

"Yeah," I said. "On the corner. Two streets down."

"Okay, " she said. "I think we'll stay by you."

She sent the young man, who happened to be her son, to get them a room. I poured the tea and the subject of my "deliverance" was not discussed again. We talked for a while and when her son returned she got ready to leave.

"We're going to the Christian Chapel tonight," she said. "Would you like to come?"

The Christian Chapel is not where you'll find me. I'm not against it—well, maybe I am—but I'm not for it either. I find their version of "spirituality" a touch too restrictive when it comes to the regions of our lesser vices.

"No," I smiled. "Not for me. But stop by in the morning and I'll have pancakes waiting."

They did, and I got the report from them.

"How was church?" I said.

"It was awful. They separated the men from the women. I felt out of place, unwelcome. I didn't care for it."

I found myself defending the place as I flipped pancakes.

"Maybe it was an off night. They can't always be inspired, can they?"

"We're going to a different one this evening—the Diamond Cathedral. Would you like to go?"

"No, most definitely not, but, I'll be around tomorrow if you'd like to take a walk."

They stayed with me a week, each night a different church, each morning another report of distance, exclusiveness, and opulence at the expense of their congregations. I felt bad for them. I took a shot.

"Would you like to see what I do?" I said. "I go to a place where they talk about God a lot—but, the Almighty might be bracketed on both ends with a "mother-fucker" or two—but it is genuine, and relatively humble and honest."

I took them to a twelve-step meeting. They loved it. They were approached and made to feel welcome. There was no one in charge. The donation basket was passed around but the take was light and there was no plea for more. The topic was forgiveness and the majority of the attendees shared their experience with the subject. It was uplifting. I felt proud of the group.

Afterwards, I needed to pick up a car. A friend had been admitted to the hospital and he needed someone to take his vehicle home. I volunteered, but I needed another driver. I asked my visitor if she'd like to come. She declined with a headache but said her son could drive and he'd be pleased to do it. Over the course of a few days the young man had opened up a bit—he was still withdrawn, but not as much as he had been upon arriving at my house.

144

We dropped off the car and then drove the coast road home. I felt uneasy, as if something needed to be said.

"Are you okay? I asked. "Your mother seems fine, but she's worried about you, there's something there. I'm not sure what but…are you okay?"

I had no reason to ask him this. There was nothing in her words that led me in this direction. She hadn't shared any intimate knowledge of herself. But I felt as if he needed something—some connection. He stared at me, almost reticent to reply and then, "Before we left home I tried to kill myself. I had been drinking, and doing drugs. The depression took me. My mother brought me to America so I could be healed."

I'm not sure if it was "God" or any other outside agent that arranged our meeting—it could have been, I have no proof either way. But I do know that I was open, and I was willing to share my life, and through learning to think properly there were now times I was divorced from selfish, self-serving notions. Because of this, I was there when he needed me.

There is a philosophy in the twelve-step program: "God" is infinite and man finite. It's a powerful thought. Basically, if we believe and invest ourselves in this source, then our troubles of the day are nothing—less than a blink of an eye—we are whole with the spirit. This philosophy transcends our fear of financial insecurity. It transcends our wants and our need for more. It transcends even death. Yes, we deal with the emotions that our physical body brings; but underneath, there is a belief that we were okay, we are okay, and we will be okay, no matter what our past, present, or future

145

situations hold—including our alcoholism. As I've said before, I don't believe in a heavenly after life—according to conventional definitions—but I do believe in consciousness and a shared energy, and this philosophy has somehow comforted me and made it easier for me to enjoy my time here.

"Very little is needed to make a happy life; it is all within yourself, in your way of thinking."

Marcus Aurelius

The Baptism of Georgia

I used to worry about my lack of faith. I thought I was damned. There were those on the program who seemed to believe without much thought and I questioned everything. It troubled me until I spoke with a friend, Reverend Leo. He told me that my lack of faith, and my discomfort with it, was a blessing that might keep me "teachable" and always yearning for a greater understanding. I think he was right.

I wanted to be baptized. I thought it might bring me closer to "God"—display my intention to Him—so I started seeking out churches. It was difficult. I didn't care for the "rocking out to Jesus" format, or what I perceived as a forced, unequivocal "love of one's neighbor" stance. I also didn't care for the stiffness and lack of soul that I saw during ceremonies. I did like the incense and the robes, but I can do that at home. The other thing that troubled me was that I've seen people healed—not just well dressed converts coming forth for deliverance, but junkies and hardcore alcoholics. I've seen the pariahs of modern day society, the social lepers baring the flesh-eating scars of addiction with nothing but space in their eyes…and I've seen them reborn. I've seen them recover and help others. I've seen them exude a spirit that was almost invisible before, and I wasn't seeing that in church. It was almost like I'd been walking around as a young man reading a *Hustler* magazine and now I was handed a *Playboy*—it just didn't have the same spark. Yet, I wanted to be baptized.

I thought about the priests I'd seen in meetings. They didn't wear their collars, but I knew who they were. I'd watched them tittering about. I figured I'd get one of them to baptize me—go back by the coffee bar and get a little dunk or something. I went back to Reverend Leo.

Leo is a throwback to the Swinging Sixties. He's a smooth dressing Englishman who, when drinking, would've fit in well with the Vegas "Rat Pack"—"Ello, darlin'. Care for a little bit of the bubbly baby?" He is an open-minded friend.

"Hey Leo," I said. "Would you baptize me?" I think my request took him a bit off-guard—I don't really act like the type who might seek this service.

"Sure, Jack," he said, "but you know anybody can baptize you."

"What? I didn't know that."

"Yes, the important thing is a desire to obey, or follow God, not who performs the act."

He got me thinking. If anybody could do it then maybe I'll get my Jewish buddy Jordan to baptize me—we could go down by the river, get some robes...I thought on this for a week and then one night, before bed, I thought of my little girl, Georgia. She was about six or seven at the time. She'd never been baptized. I walked into the kitchen and I put water in a bowl. I asked God to bless it.

"You know what I want to do with this Father," I said. "Please make it so." I walked into my daughter's room. She was lying on top of her bunk bed—blonde hair and a splash of freckles—watching her videos.

"Hey G?" I said. "Can I talk to you about God?"

She rolled over on her stomach and leaned up against the rail.

"Sure," she said—exposing a missing tooth. "What's up?"

148

"Do you know that you're loved, and that God loves you?"

"Yeah sure."

"Do you know that we're all a family and it's our job to look after others? Do you know that that's why Dad brings people home and helps them get back on their feet?"

"Yeah."

"And do you know that we're all God's children—plenty of love."

"Yeah Dad. I know."

I held up the bowl with the water.

"Do you mind if I mark you as one of God's kids? Would you like that?"

She leaned forward. I dipped my fingers into the water and I touched them to her forehead. She closed her eyes.

"Sweetheart, I baptize you in the name of the Father, the Son, and the Holy Spirit," I pulled her closer and I gave her a kiss. "Good night G. I love you."

I turned to walk away—reached for the door, and then her voice like blossoms fell behind me.

"Pops," she said. "Can I do you?"

I turned toward her—shaking, I held out the bowl, the water as clear and as pure as any I'd ever seen. She dipped her fingers into the bowl. I leaned forward as she touched my forehead.

"Father," she said, "I baptize you in the name of the Father, the Son, and the Holy Spirit." She said it perfectly, without hesitation, and then she dropped her hand to my neck, pulled me close, kissed me and said, "I love you. Goodnight."

Two weeks later she came to me as I sat smoking in the yard.

149

"You know, Pops?" she touched her forehead. "I can still feel it."

An agnostic is one who believes that nothing is known or can be known of God—there is no faith in that above material phenomena. And, while I've spoken of God, implored God's help, and told you tales of interaction with a force unseen, there is nothing that has happened to me to change my beliefs—or my doubts.

"The 'Kingdom of Heaven' is a condition of heart—not something that comes 'upon the earth' or 'after death.'"
Nietzsche

In All Our Affairs

Sometimes I get frustrated with the program. Not the steps, or our beautiful traditions, but with us—a shitload of controlling egotistical alcoholics that think "their" way is the right path to sobriety and "God". And, let's make this perfectly clear: the steps are designed to reacquaint, introduce, or encourage you to find that inner resource. Bill writes on pg. 95 of the Big Book, "...if he is to find God the desire must come from within."

"What? If his desire is to find God...but I thought this was about getting sober?"

Really? You thought this was about "getting" sober? Show me in the book where it tells you how to quit? Where's the chapter to the man who is still hammered? I'm still looking for the section in big print that reads one word to a page: Put—That—Shit—Down. It's not in there. There are no steps for tapering off. Step One isn't: get enough booze for the weekend. Step Two: shut off the phone. Step Three: begin to taper... The program is for those who are done, and don't ever want to go back to drinking or getting loaded again. Not one day at a time—although emotionally that's how we work through our lives—but to be done for good and for all.

Some have said in meetings that if you don't have this experience or that one, then you haven't really worked these steps; that if you don't say it like this, do it like we do, then you're not really one of us. I've heard people fight over line and verse as if

"God" was in the words. It's sickening, the amount of pride and control that goes into that kind of talk, and I wonder how many people these "perfect program workers" have run out of our groups.

"Oh, bullshit, Jack. If we run them out, the booze will run them back."

"Really? You believe that? You walk around spouting off all this fatal illness crap and yet you think the booze will 'run them back'? I'd suggest a reality check. I know many people who were driven from our program and never made it back. But I guess they don't count, right? 'They were too sick to stay.'"

I lead a group on Saturday nights called, "Conversations with a Drunk"—if you're ever in Long Beach stop by and see us. The meeting is conducted in an interview style and the premise is, a long-timer—someone over twenty-five years sober—and myself, or another host, sit on a couple of barstools and we talk about sobriety as a few hundred people listen in. Our guest is encouraged not to give "their pitch" as many circuit speakers do, but instead, they are asked to answer questions about their journey within the program. "How did you get to us? What's the first thing you identified with? Did you immediately, or at any time, get a sponsor? Were you, or are you, comfortable with God?" We aren't interested in a twelve-step show; we want the truth, unvarnished and real. We usually get it. There are times we can't stop laughing—I've been called Oprah and have been teased about my nervous disposition—it does get a trifle hot up there. At other times we've cried or become quite misty-eyed as one of our members opens up to a hurt that's not usually shared from the podium—they often take us somewhere deeper than we expected. We've had known speakers put aside their usual tale and focus on one aspect of their story, like losing face within the group, or acting out on a certain defect of character which cost them everything but their sobriety. The meeting has been in existence for three years and guess what? We have never heard the same story twice, one hundred fifty-six guests, well over four thousand years of sobriety, and each journey through the steps is a touch different. Before the meeting starts we read this statement.

"God forbid that 'our program' ever becomes frozen or rigid in its ways of doing or thinking. Within the framework of our principles the ways are apparently legion."

That passage is from a letter Bill wrote in 1949. For those of you who attend meetings could you imagine the response this statement would get today—if one of ours were to stand up and say that there is a multitude of ways to work these steps, that there is no "right" way? They'd be run from some groups, or branded as a subversive, or someone who was altering the program to fit their own needs.

Every one of our previous guest speakers conceded to their innermost selves and admitted they were powerless. They all sought out a Higher Power or an enlightened self. They took inventory—some used the lines and columns, some like Dr. Bob invoked a story-telling style, while others took a more autobiographical approach. We've even had a few speakers claim the old "matchbook" route, where you actually write your inventory on the back of a book of matches; but they all looked within using one form or another. They also made amends—no two the same. These one hundred fifty-six guests have eloquently shown our group how

153

they do some sort of a daily inventory, and that they are fresh, vibrant, giving people who live lives full of love and service. By the way, we've had quite a few agnostic guests who, although neither deny nor believe in the existence of God, have worked these steps and are as happy and as useful as the most fervent believer.

Step Twelve reads:

"Having had a spiritual awakening as the result of these steps, we tried to carry this message to alcoholics, and to practice these principles in all our affairs."

"A spiritual awakening as the result of these steps, hmm?"

When do you think you're going to wake up? Do you think you can "pen and paper" your way to "God"? Do you think you're going to somehow be beamed into space when you hit Step Twelve? What do you think a spiritual awakening is?

I believe a spiritual awakening is when you first realize that there is someone here besides you, and that their lives are just as important as yours, not less or more. You're awake when you realize that other people have their own plans and ideas, and that you don't have to agree to or oppose them. I believe you're awake when the care of others becomes a primary concern—when you think beyond your immediate environment and let your thoughts travel to all of those who inhabit our world. I believe you're awake when you realize that their triumphs are yours and their abuse, their discord, and their suffering diminishes you as well.

Now, if you're awake, what is the message you carry? Is it just sobriety? I know that if I had initially heard that message I wouldn't have been too happy. Sobriety sucked. I hurt worse sober than I

154

ever did when I was drunk. When I was sedated I was good to go, but I couldn't stay that way. It didn't work. I'd get sober, life wouldn't behave, I'd seek the "ease and comfort" of the bottle, a touch of weed or a few pills, and then I'd overdo it, create chaos, get sober, and then get uncomfortable again. You know the pattern. So, what's your message? Don't tell me that you're going to regurgitate some "depth and weight" from the book, because I'll see through that—your message must be more than your words. Yes, I want to hear about freedom, love, and power, but I also want to look in your eyes and see the spark of those words manifested. I want to hear the language of the heart and that involves a tone that flows beneath the sound of your voice—a tone you can't fake. I want your message to be in your actions, in the way you stand, offer assistance, and smile. When I see you I want to see a painting splashed with life, not a print of your sponsor's or your grand-sponsor's life—I want to see *yours* with all its faults, imperfections, assets, glory and uniqueness. Anyone can repeat a phrase, but a message is different; a message is a discrete unit of communication—individually separate and distinct. In other words, I'd rather see a sermon than hear one.

A principle is a code of conduct to which we hold firm, to the best of our ability, no matter the circumstance. We practice love and service—that is our main principle of recovery—in all of our affairs.

I have been around drugs and alcohol for as long as I've been sober. A fellow musician once joked with me, "You know we sell booze for a living?" I laughed, but he's right. I play in a punk rock band and the clubs, who have us as guests, count on us to play well and long, so they can crank out heavy bar sales. I don't give a fuck. It's none of my business what they do. I don't care who drinks

155

either, that's also none of my business. Bill writes on pg. 103, "We are careful never to show intolerance or hatred of drinking as an institution…a spirit of intolerance might repel alcoholics whose lives could have been saved, had it not been for such stupidity." You bet your ass. I know this better than most. Don't attack, criticize, or talk down to another who is doing their best. Instead, be there when they need help. Be open about being clean but make sure they know that their lives are their own—not ours.

The phrase "saving lives"…well, that sounds a touch grandiose to me. I'd never say, "I saved your life" to someone, but I can see how this program has—and not just through sobriety, but through sharing our selves.

I was on tour—ten of us riding in a family camper van that was not meant for hard pop-tunes and anarchistic leanings. We were in Florida. When I travel I go to meetings, and if I don't have time to attend, I at least call the local "Central Office" and get an address and a place. Once again, I don't need meetings, but I enjoy them. I like the people there—I'm one who actually enjoys drunks, wet or dry, and you can normally hear a good, positive message in the rooms. I've been to meetings all over the world. It's beautiful to see and feel the connection first hand…

"Okay, Jack. Hang on. You said that you've been around booze the whole time you've been clean? You go to bars and hang out with people who are still drinking? It doesn't bother you?"

"No. It doesn't. What part of 'thoroughly convinced' didn't you get? I've been restored to sanity. I've connected with a Power

156

Greater than myself. I no longer have an alcoholic mind. I'm not powerless."

"Ah, that's it, *now we caught you*—you cocky fucker. You aren't powerless? You no longer have an alcoholic mind? Should we wait until you relapse or pour you one now?"

"Well, I was in the middle of a story but, just for the hell of it I'll throw you a few more Big Book quotes before I get back to Florida."

Here we go—straight from the Big Book:

"As we felt new power flow in, as we enjoyed peace of mind, as we discovered we could face life successfully, as we became conscious of His presence, we began to lose our fear of today, tomorrow or the hereafter. We were reborn." Pg. 63

You bet—I'm conscious, awake, aware and able to feel the connection that flows through humankind. I've been reborn. I'm a man whose whole outlook on life has changed. A few years ago I wrote a novel called *An American Demon*. If you'd like to read about the man I was, feel free to do so, but I warn you…it won't go down like a warm cup of cocoa on a cool winter evening. It's terrifying. I've had some tell me they couldn't finish it because it was so upsetting. It also ends where I got clean and I've been asked, "Why?" "Why didn't you go on to a happy ending?" My reply is always the same, "Because, the man that book is about died. I'm not him. I have become a new creation and resemble him but little."

"That is the miracle of it. We are not fighting it, neither are we avoiding temptation. We feel as though we had been placed in a position of neutrality—safe and protected. We have not even sworn

157

off. Instead, the problem has been removed. It does not exist for us. We are neither cocky nor are we afraid. That is our experience. That is how we react so long as we keep in fit spiritual condition." Pg. 85

I don't care about booze or any of the rest of it. I don't want a "freebie" at the dentist and I don't fantasize about what the latest adult beverage tastes like. My friend Tom, sober over fifty years, says he could wash his car with a bucket of booze—expensive, and he's joking, but the bottom line is: there's just no more power left in the sauce. As for being spiritually fit, what does that mean? It means I'm not wrapped up in "self". I'm not angry and I'm not acting out on any of those character defects that I've been known to indulge in. I know what's around me. When I walk into a bar, or when I'm with a friend who might be having a drink, I'm aware that I'm surrounded by poison. I'm careful. If I order a soda or something else, I don't gulp it down without smelling it first—bottled water is a good choice.

"Assuming we are spiritually fit, we can do all sorts of things alcoholics are not supposed to do. People have said we must not go where liquor is served; we must not have it in our homes; we must shun friends who drink; we must avoid moving pictures which show drinking scenes; we must not go into bars; our friends must hide their bottles if we go to their houses; we mustn't think or be reminded about alcohol at all. Our experience shows that this is not necessarily so. We meet these conditions every day. An alcoholic who cannot meet them, still has an alcoholic mind; there is something the matter with his spiritual status." Pg. 101

I've heard too many old-timers who sit in meetings and talk about their "alcoholic mind". Hey guys, if you've been sober that long and the bitch called "booze" still owns you, you should get a chain collar that reads, "slave". I go wherever I want without fear. Now, am I hanging out with people who are blacking out, smoking speed, shooting dope, or selling weed? No, of course not. Am I a friend to those who are in the depths of their illness, inflicting pain on their families, committing crimes, and diving headlong into the alcoholic bliss? You bet, a friend yes, a road-dog no. I'm here if, and when, they need me. At times I'll reach out, a phone call or a drive by, but they don't have anything I want. I don't find the lifestyle attractive and unless you enjoy drama the conversation is less than stimulating.

"Your job now is to be at the place where you may be of maximum helpfulness to others, so never hesitate to go anywhere if you can be helpful. You should not hesitate to visit the most sordid spot on earth on such an errand. Keep on the firing line of life with these motives and God will keep you unharmed." Pg. 102

"The most sordid spot on earth?" The Big Book must be talking about some of the stops on my last tour. I've played in places that were condemned months before we arrived. I've slept rolled-up in the car rather than sleep on beds crawling with bugs, and I've walked streets that the darkest angels refused to stroll. You bet. I go in. I go

as me—a sober, life-loving punk, and I cherish the adventure. Every so often, I find myself in these places for reasons unrelated to my own devices. I'm not there for me. I'm there for the alcoholic who needs to see that quitting drinking isn't the end—it's the beginning. Now, if you don't mind, let's go back to Florida...

So I'm sitting in a meeting. It's held in a small clubhouse building surrounded by mangroves and ferns—a quintessential Florida panhandle locale. I'm with the boys in the band and we don't have a show for a few days so we're kind of dicking around. The meeting starts and the shares are pretty standard, for the most part, full of solution and uplifting, but then...one of the members starts relating a tale of woe. It was one of those shares where you could tell that the guy talking was about a bullet or a rope close to the edge. He even said, "I can't take it anymore. Sobriety sucks. I'm through." Guys like this aren't going to listen to words. When you get locked up in that cage of self-pity there isn't much anyone can do for you— unless they grab you by the hand and walk you out. I approached him after the meeting.

"Hey man," I said. "What's up?"

He looked at me a touch wary and I don't blame him—my hair was blue and unsolicited advice is the plague that flows from the mouths of too many in recovery. But I don't give advice.

"Fuckin A, huh?" I said. "You're gonna take yourself out, yeah?"

He dropped his shoulders and looked me straight in the eyes with no hope—sober, he wasn't drinking, but he wasn't living.

"What do you care?" he said.

"I don't know," I said, "but why don't you come with me, I'm driving around with a van full of crazies and we're all clean. Come on. You're going to kill yourself anyway. Give me a few days."

Now, I can immediately tell who the whiners and the attention seekers are—their primary defect of character involves sounding

160

pitiful so they can get a little scrap of "Oh, don't worry baby, it's gonna be okay." But this cat wasn't one of those. He was the real deal. He looked at me, drifting on the edge between life and death, and then he teetered in my direction.

"Okay," he said. "I'll go. Can we go by my place and grab some clothes and shit?"

"No," I said. "You come as you are. Fuck your place. You're dead anyway. Go get in the van."

He did, and since we were on tour, we dragged that crazy fucker all over Florida and up the East Coast. We went to meetings. We rented a speedboat and dove a coral reef, and we lived. He saw that a sober life could be amazing—not through words, no Big Book pages, no promise of a Holy place after death—it was right here, right now, and it was great. He was with us a bit over a week. When we reached New York, he took his leave.

"Thanks, man," he said as he jumped from the van. He walked around to the driver's window and then he smiled at me. "I get it," he said. "I'm in."

He's still sober today—twenty years later, married, and living a dream that has taken him all over the world.

Often times we think we need the perfect words. We stutter over what we should've said or done…but we don't need to. Sometimes—shit, most of the time—all we have to do is be willing to stick out a hand, to let the power within flow through, and to humbly share ourselves. If you're awake, reborn, and alive, people will see it. Words are beautiful, and they're fun to play with, but they're nothing but icing on the sweet dessert of the spirit.

On a seaside mountain above the Pacific Ocean, near the town of St. Lucia is a monastery. A meeting is held there, or at least one used to be. This area of Big Sur is breathtaking and beautiful. The waves in winter often roll reckless over the coast road. It's wild, desolate, and a wonderful place to search for God. My nephew and I drove up to the monastery one afternoon, via a steep hand swept road held in place by redwoods and fog. The hermitage was hidden above the clouds. Our connection was Brother John—a recluse there. When we arrived he was seated on a bench in a large, round, cedar-lined room, invested in quiet meditation—part of a group of monks bathing in incense and solitude. He was happy to see us, as it was rare that outsiders came to his meeting—the attendants usually consisted of him and Brother Tom. We walked quietly toward an outer building. The sun sent random, staggering rays of light through the clouds and touched our path. The room we entered had windows on all sides offering a divine, limitless view from the mountaintop. We sat in a circle, respectful yet close. A moment of silence was observed, although we had said little by way of conversation. On the grass outside three mule deer appeared, grazing without fear. The serenity prayer was softly said:

"God, grant me the serenity to accept the things I cannot change, the courage to change the things I can, and the wisdom to know the difference."

John assumed leadership of our group. "First," he said, "I'd like to thank you for coming—we appreciate your company." He was bathed in sunlight as he spoke, and I knew that I had finally arrived.

"This is it," I thought. "This is where I'll get my answers. This is what I've been waiting for."

"Okay," Brother John said, "Who'd like to begin?"

162

My soul was perched to soar, to finally climb above the humanity where I'd been sent to wallow in and hurt. This is where I'll step beyond the pursuits of self. This is where I'll transverse this life and fly. Brother Tom raised his hand.

"Okay," he said. "I guess I'll go. Fuck Brother Frank, he's not doing his chores."

Made in the USA
Middletown, DE
26 November 2015